Daily Splashes of Joy

Daily Splashes of Joy

Barbara Johnson

WORD PUBLISHING

NASHVILLE

A Thomas Nelson Company

Acknowledgments

I HOPE YOU ENJOY the daily devotions and cartoons in this volume. Most have been adapted from my previously published books. The quips and one-liners have come from the many letters and clippings shared with me by friends and supporters of Spatula Ministries, and in many cases the sources are unknown. Some were borrowed from Edythe Draper, *Draper's Book of Quotations for the Christian World* (Tyndale House Publishers, 1992) and Lowell D. Streiker's two books, *An Encyclopedia of Humor* (Hendrickson Publishers, 1998) and *Nelson's Big Book of Laughter* (Thomas Nelson, 2000). In addition, my thanks go to these friends and organizations for allowing me to reuse their materials:

Don Addis, the *St. Petersburg* (Florida) *Times,* for the cartoon depicting the "Fighting Methuselahs" at Sunset Manor Nursing Facility.

"Ten to One" (April 13) from *Tell Me Again, Lord, I Forget,* © 1974, and the poem "I Don't Understand" (October 16) from *Lord, It Keeps Happening and Happening,* © 1984, both by Ruth Harms Calkin, Pomona, CA 91768. Used by permission. All rights reserved.

Mary Chambers's witty cartoon (August 4) is reprinted from her book *Church Is Stranger Than Fiction,* © 1990 by Mary Chambers. Used by permission of Inter-Varsity Press, P.O. Box 1400, Downers Grove, Illinois 60515.

Ron and Karen Grosse, Lighthouse Christian Books in Green Bay, Wisconsin, for their insightful photo of the flood-damaged neighborhood.

Darcey Hripak for her adorable little characters depicting the "wardrobe" of Colossians 3:12–14.

The Lion magazine, Lions Clubs International, for the cartoon, "You are here . . . because your husband won't ask for directions."

Danny Loya for his thought-provoking illustration of shoes related to 1 Corinthians 15:52.

And special thanks to cartoonists Randy Glasbergen, Bunny Hoest, Bil Keane, John McPherson, and Dana Summers for granting permission for me to include their witty works in these pages.

Splashing Each Day with Joy

OH, THAT WE ALL might have the happy demeanor of an old lady in the nursing home where my sister, Janet, visits to play the piano for the residents. One week the feisty, ninety-three-year-old woman told Janet, "I wake up in the morning, sit on the edge of the bed, put my feet on the floor, and say to myself, 'I know who I am . . . I know what day it is. And then I say, 'Well, PRAISE the Lord!'"

Starting each morning with an attitude of gratitude—no matter what the circumstances—can splash joy over the rest of your day. The moment your eyelids flutter open, remind yourself to whisper the old lady's jubilant prayer: *Praise the Lord!* Say it out loud with a smile on your face, and you might just be surprised at the difference it makes in your morning.

Force yourself to smile as you make your way to the bathroom so that when you catch a glimpse of yourself in the mirror, you're ready for that first laugh of the day. (This may be easier for some of you than others, depending on what appears in that mirror!) Look for joy gems sparkling in all the dark corners as the hours pass.

Sometimes the smallest word or the most unlikely gesture of kindness is all that's needed to turn a hurting heart toward the light of God's love. I know how often a friend's joke or funny story has helped *me* find the silver lining in an otherwise gloomy day. I hope the same thing happens as you work your way through this book of daily readings. May you be encouraged by the thoughts, jokes, cartoons, and suggestions included here. They're my way of sharing a splash of joy with you each morning! I hope each little gem lifts your spirits all day long, until you finally lay your head on your pillow again at night, still smiling as you remember the moment we shared.

It's not always easy to be joyful. But it's possible, because as Christians we have a secret strength—we have hope! And we know the rewards of joy-seeking are always worth the effort, because as soon as we decide to be joy-*seekers* we turn into joy-*spreaders*. Then the joy we share with others boomerangs back to splash us with refreshment. As Christians, we are *all* blessed to be a blessing.

Joy!

Barb

The LORD spoke to Moses and Aaron in the land of Egypt: "This month will be the beginning of months, the first month of the year for you." (EXODUS 12:1–2 NCV)

There's something so satisfying about beginning a new month. I just love r-r-r-ripping that old page off my calendar and starting over on a fresh, new month with all those clean, unblemished squares—unspoiled days just waiting to be enjoyed. Celebrating the first of the month is one of my longtime traditions. On that day I change the sheets, wash my hair, and take a bath (on other days too, of course, but especially on the first of the month). Then I do something special—like treat myself to asparagus! But the most important thing I do is resolve (again) to heed the apostle Paul's advice: Forgetting all the pain and failures of the past, I strain toward what is ahead—heaven!—and I put the future in God's hands.

The present is what slips by us while we're pondering the past and worrying about the future.

January 2

A relaxed attitude lengthens a man's life.
(PROVERBS 14:30 TLB)

Some people spread joy wherever they go—whether or not they mean to! And some of us have to put forth a little effort to keep a smile in our hearts. Others are never happy unless they're complaining about something. I got a note from a woman who had a friend like that. Luckily, the woman who wrote to me could see the humor even in having such a pessimistic friend. She wrote, "My friend Irene is always complaining! I took her to a greeting-card store the other day, and she looked and looked and looked.

"Finally, I said, 'Irene, what in the world are you looking for?'

"She replied, 'I'm looking for a card that says, "I had what you've got—only WORSE!"'"

This is the same witty woman who told me her horoscope predicted one morning that she was going to have an adventure involving water. "And then," she continued, "I dropped my false teeth in the toilet!"

I am wonderful, marvelous, extraspecial, unique, first-rate, exceptional, outrageous, surprising, superlative—and, above all, HUMBLE.

The LORD is my strength and my song; he has become my salvation. . . . The LORD is a warrior; the LORD is his name. (EXODUS 15:2–3)

Hardening of the heart ages people more quickly than hardening of the arteries.

January 4

Delight yourself in the LORD and he will give you the
desires of your heart. (PSALM 37:4)

I talk to many gals who go through the year without receiving a nice, gift-wrapped present with their own name on it. There is a fabulous remedy for this problem. Right after the first of the year (when most stores have sales) find a store that sells nice little gifts and does courtesy gift-wrapping. Pick out at least five presents for yourself to cover your birthday, Valentine's Day, Mother's Day, wedding anniversary, and Christmas. They needn't be costly, but they should be something you like.

Bring your presents home and place them around the house in prominent spots where you'll have to move them as you clean. That way they get shifted around so much you'll forget what is in which package. Then each one is a surprise when you open it! This idea works beautifully. When anyone asks you what your husband gave you for your birthday or anniversary or your kids gave you for Mother's Day, you can proudly show them the lovely gift that you "received." (You don't have to tell *everything* you know!)

Life is a gift. Unwrap your present!

He who is of a merry heart has a continual feast.
(PROVERBS 15:15 NKJV)

One day I noticed a car parked at the La Habra post office with a license plate that said, "2 BUM NEZ." I thought, *That's so cute—the guy probably has arthritis or something.*

As I tore around the car with my arms full of things to mail, I called out, "Oh, I just LOVE your license plate!" Someone was helping him out of the car and suddenly I saw that he didn't have any legs! Talk about hoof-and-mouth disease! But he put me at ease by saying, "I'm glad you like it. My wife said I should get one that says, 'NO LEGS,' but I would rather have folks get a chuckle out of it like you did than have them feel sorry for me."

I love that dear man's attitude. It beautifully illustrates one of my favorite mottoes: *Pain is inevitable but misery is optional!*

May all your troubles last as long as your New Year's resolutions.

January 6

How well he understands us and knows what is best for us at all times. (EPHESIANS 1:8 TLB)

It was one of those days when everything had gone wrong. Preparing to leave town for a speaking engagement, I hurried to the supermarket to stock up on a few things I would need for the trip. Naturally, I got a *dumb* basket with wheels going in different directions. As I made my way to the checkout counter, I felt completely forsaken when I saw the checkout line filled with women who apparently were shopping for the U.S. Army.

"Please, Lord!" I prayed. "I need just a LITTLE encouragement today."

Just then a man stepped into an empty checkout stand and said, "Young lady, I'll be glad to check you out over here!"

I looked around. Then I looked at the clerk. Why, he was talking to *me!*

Maybe it was the *young lady* part that lifted my spirits. But mostly I think it was knowing I wasn't forsaken. I believe he opened that line *just for me*. What a simple way to be reminded of God's continual care.

Frogs have it easy. They can **eat** *what's bugging them!*

Be truly glad! There is wonderful joy ahead, even though the going is rough for a while down here. These trials are only to test your faith. (1 PETER 1:6 TLB)

We can hope for a miracle, but there is no simple, quick way to be young, thin, and lovely. As the years zoom by, you begin to think you're in a war to keep your mind together, your body functioning, your teeth in, your hair on, and your weight off. It can really be a chore. It's a lot like trying to hold a beachball under water . . . sooner or later something pops up or out! That's why my favorite excuse is, "I used to be Snow White . . . but I drifted!"

Aging gracefully means living long enough to make a joke of the things that were once breaking your heart.

January 8

Come to me, all you who are weary and burdened, and I will give you rest. (Matthew 11:28)

Tears and heartaches come to us all. They are part of living, but Jesus Christ can ease the heartache. Give God the pain and sorrow; give Him the guilt you feel.

And remember, you are not alone; many are in God's waiting room for what seems like forever, learning lessons, suffering pain, and growing. But the fertilizer that helps us grow is in those valleys, not on the mountaintops.

The iron crown of suffering precedes the golden crown of glory. Real, genuine healing is a process. It takes a long time for deep hurts to be resolved.

No, life isn't always what you want, but it's what you've got; so, with God's help, CHOOSE TO BE HAPPY.

Laughter is the invisible armor to protect us from the stresses of life.

He who refreshes others will himself be refreshed.
(PROVERBS 11:25)

One of my Bible heroes is Onesiphorus, the man who the apostle Paul said, "often refreshed me and was not ashamed of my chains" (2 Timothy 1:16). He encouraged Paul when the aging apostle was weary and lonely by letting him know there was still someone who cared. *The Living Bible* translation says Onesiphorus's visits revived Paul "like a breath of fresh air."

Sure, Onesiphorus is a somewhat obscure character. He's only mentioned once in the entire Bible—and his name sounds like a disease, to boot! But when I get to heaven, I'm going to look him up and tell him I've spent a great part of my life trying to be like him.

A friend is one who strengthens you with prayers, blesses you with love, and encourages you with hope.

January 10

I trust in you, O LORD; I say, "You are my God." My times are in your hands. (PSALM 31:14–15)

I was on a plane one time reading Billy Graham's book *Facing Death and the Life Hereafter*. The person in the seat next to me said, "Oh, what an awful book you're reading—how depressing!"

I just laughed and said, "It's not depressing. It's exciting. It's a wonderful book."

"Do you have cancer or something?" he asked.

I explained that we all have an incurable disease with a high mortality rate. It's called *life*. We're *all* going to die. We're on our way out of here, and it's a one-way trip. Billy Graham's book reminds us why Christians can face death with joy, not gloom. Facing death is really the ultimate triumph for a Christian.

Whatever problems we're going through, they didn't come to stay; they "came to pass." And that helps us cope, whether it's cancer or problems in our marriages or with our children. We know that what's up ahead is going to be glorious because of the hope we have as Christians.

This bumper sticker explains why I'm a perpetual failure at dieting: *EAT RIGHT, STAY FIT . . . DIE ANYWAY!*

I find rest in God; only he gives me hope.
(PSALM 62:5 NCV)

As we finally let go of a loved one who has died, we move into the last part of our "grief work." This doesn't mean we become our old selves again. We will *never* be our old selves again. We come out of any kind of deep grief as different persons than we were before. We can come out stronger, kinder, and more understanding of the problems of others, or we can come out bitter and self-pitying, uninterested in others' problems because we have too many of our own. Experts say the people who cope best with deep grief have a deep faith; God and His love are very real to them.

I read somewhere that the future has two handles. We can take hold of tomorrow by the handle of anxiety or by the handle of faith, and . . .

If you grasp tomorrow with faith, you know the handle won't fall off!

I will forget my complaint; I will change the look on my face and smile. (JOB 9:27 NCV)

Smiles are everywhere if you just take the trouble to look. No only does smiling kill time between disasters, but it also helps your attitude—and you know we *all* have to work to avoid hardening of the attitudes!

Actually, it isn't all that difficult to have a cheerful attitude. As someone said in the following quip, you just have to grin and bear it:

Life is easier than you think. All you have to do is: Accept the impossible, do without the indispensable, bear the intolerable, and be able to smile at anything.

Joy comes in our lives when we have something to do, something to love, and something to hope for.

*Don't worry about anything; instead, pray about
everything; tell God your needs and don't forget to thank
him for his answers.* (PHILIPPIANS 4:6 TLB)

There will be times when we lose the luster in our lives, and it is vital to know how to restore it. When silver or brass becomes tarnished, we get out the tarnish remover and do some rubbing. What can we do when we need to bring back the shine in our own lives? We can pause early in the day to seek God's guidance. We can count our blessings and name them one by one.

An attitude of gratitude rids our lives of the film of frustration, the rust of resentment, and the varnish of vanity—all destroyers of self-esteem. When we count our blessings, we multiply harmony and good feelings, and the lamp's flame burns higher once again.

Without God's touch in our lives—His work in us to will and to do His good pleasure—there is no sparkle. But when we allow Him to work within us—when we feel His hand upon us—we are no longer hidden treasures; we become sparkling jewels that beautify His kingdom.

Thank You, dear God, for all You have given me, all You have taken away from me, and for all You have left me!

January 14

I have great joy and comfort, my brother, because the love you have shown to God's people has refreshed them.
(PHILEMON 7 NCV)

When a bit of sunshine hits ye,
After passing of a cloud,
When a bit of laughter gits ye
An' yer spine is feelin' proud,
Don't forgit to up and flight it
At a soul that's feelin' blue
For the minit that ye sling it
It's a boomerang to you!

—CAPT. JACK CRAWFORD, 1913

The blessings that come from reaching out to others cannot be overestimated.

Let us not become weary in doing good, for at the proper time we will reap a harvest if we do not give up.
(GALATIANS 6:9)

Friends help us by their willingness to laugh at the goofiness that unexpectedly pops into our lives to brighten the dark places. One woman wrote to describe how her friend gave her a laugh as she was recovering from cancer. Chemotherapy had caused the woman to lose her hair, so she wore a wig. Later, her friend was helping her "get back together" as she came out of the recovery room after surgery:

She put my wig on me, and when I reached up to see if it was OK, . . . I said, "Marge, you've got it backwards."

She said, "Are you sure?"

I said, "Yes, my bangs don't curl upwards!"

I tell everyone I'm sure glad she didn't try to put in my false teeth!

Laughter dulls the sharpest pain and flattens out the greatest stress. To share it is to give a gift of health, because, as someone pointed out:

Ulcers can't grow while you're laughing.

January 16

On the day I called to you, you answered me.
You made me strong and brave. (PSALM 138:3 NCV)

"I would have been here sooner,
but I got hooked on oat bran muffins."

If at first you don't succeed . . .
see if the loser gets anything.

The Lamb . . . will be their shepherd; he will lead them to springs of living water. And God will wipe away every tear from their eyes. (REVELATION 7:17)

Y*ou say,* "It's impossible." God says, "All things are possible" (Luke 18:27).

You say, "I can't go on." God says, "I will direct your steps" (Proverbs 3:5–6).

You say, "I'm not able." God says, "I am able" (2 Corinthians 9:8).

You say, "I can't forgive myself." God says, "I forgive you!" (1 John 1:9; Romans 8:1).

You say, "I'm afraid." God says, "Do not be afraid, little flock" (Luke 12:32).

You say, "I'm so worried." God says, "Give all your worries to Me" (1 Peter 5:7).

You say, "I feel so alone." God says, "I will never leave you or forsake you" (Hebrews 13:5).

I write down everything I want to remember. That way, instead of spending a lot of time trying to remember what I wrote down, I spend time looking for the paper I wrote it down on. —PAT HANSEN

January 18

Pray continually. (1 Thessalonians 5:17 NCV)

Someone sent me this simple way to remember to pray for myself and others—the five-finger prayer:

1. When your clasp your hands in prayer, your thumb is closest to you. Begin your prayer by remembering those closest to you—your children, parents, friends, and other loved ones.

2. The pointing finger is next. Pray for those who point the way: teachers, ministers, and mentors.

3. The tallest finger reminds us to pray for our leaders in government, business, schools, and churches.

4. The ring finger is actually our weakest finger. Pray for those who are sick or in trouble. Ask God to show them that they are weak but He is strong.

5. The smallest finger reminds us that we are to put others before ourselves, even in prayer. By the time we have prayed for the needs of the four other groups of people, our own needs will probably seem much less important. The little finger reminds us to pray for ourselves—and to hold to the Bible's promise that "the least shall be the greatest among you."

The glory of each morning is that it offers us a chance to begin again.

Consider the lilies of the field, how they grow; they toil not, neither do they spin: And yet I say unto you, That even Solomon in all his glory was not arrayed like one of these. (MATTHEW 6:28–29 KJV)

Memo:
  Remind me to tell you about
  the plans I have for your
  life. —By the way,
  they're plans to give you a
  future and a hope.
                        God
  (Jeremiah 29)

Lord Jesus Christ, You are the journey, the journey's end, the journey's beginning. —DEAN MAYNE

January 20

Then I heard the voice of the Lord saying, "Whom shall I send? And who will go for us?" And I said, "Here am I. Send me!" (ISAIAH 6:8)

Many older women, especially those who suddenly find themselves alone, hesitate trying something new because they might look foolish. Thank heaven for braver souls—like the lady who helped her church raise money for a new building. At a service auction, she sold eight singing telegrams, which she merrily "delivered" for the purchasers. She says:

> Soon I began receiving calls. I went to the post office for a sixtieth birthday. To the park for an aunt's eightieth. To a nursing home to sing for a mother. . . . The more I went out the sillier I dressed. . . . Everyone received me so graciously and I had great fun. Laughter brings such blessings!

This darling gal probably felt foolish the first time she arrived at the post office and announced she was going to SING for someone! But she overcame her fears and shared a blessing.

There is hope for any woman who can look in a mirror and laugh at what she sees.

For a thousand years in thy sight are but as yesterday when it is past, and as a watch in the night. (PSALM 90:4 KJV)

Today is filled with hurried hustle-bustle, and tomorrow is a mystery, but our yesterdays are treasures from the past to be cherished and enjoyed again and again. These treasures create a colorful, firmly woven tapestry of memories. The happy times are the golden threads that catch the sunlight, warming the soul. The bright pattern was created by our loved ones—parents or siblings, children and grandchildren. The black, somber woof threads that subdue the tapestry's gaudiness were painstakingly woven in hardships. Some threads are frayed. Others are broken. But the tapestry remains intact because other threads, as invisible as love yet as strong as the everlasting arms, are woven among the weakened ones.

I think of how we wove our way through joys and sorrow, glorying in each other's triumphs and supporting each other in times of trial. And in every loop and knot of our lives, I see the hand of God.

We all know why women who are over fifty don't have babies. They would put them down someplace and forget where they left them!

So this is what the Lord GOD says to them: I, myself, will judge between the fat sheep and the thin sheep. . . . I will save my flock; they will not be hurt anymore. (EZEKIEL 34:20, 22 NCV)

Ewes not fat

Ewes just fluffy

The second day of a diet is always easier than the first. By the second day you're off it.

Blessed is the man who perseveres under trial, because when he has stood the test, he will receive the crown of life that God has promised to those who love him.
(JAMES 1:12)

It's impossible to feel miserable while imagining ourselves wearing the crown Jesus has promised us and saying, "Thank You, God!" It's just as hard to stick a perky geranium in your hat and be gloomy! If you're not bold enough to do it literally, you can at least do it in your imagination. Just envision yourself, no matter what your circumstances, joyfully adorned with a silly hat or a heavenly crown. And let your first words of the morning be, "Thank You, God!"

What fun it was to stand at the podium in a church where I'd been invited to speak and look out over a sea of zaniness. The "ticket" to get in that day was to wear some kind of crazy hat. The idea that stole the show was one woman's portrayal of laughter in life's cesspools. On her head she wore an upside-down bedpan, decorated with geraniums!

I give you my life. Save me, LORD, God of truth. . . . I will be glad and rejoice in your love, because you saw my suffering; you knew my troubles. (PSALM 31:5, 7 NCV)

Pain is inevitable, but misery is optional. Adversity will come. The winds of torment will sting your face. The storms of life will almost bury you. Remember . . . sometimes God calms the storm, and sometimes He lets the storm rage and calms His child.

No matter what kind of stress threatens to overwhelm you, you can survive and be a winner. As somebody said, "Hallelujah, we win! I read the back of the book, and WE WIN!"

Above all, God always keeps His promises! Whatever the stress you're facing right now, you WILL get through it. You will win, and after you're a winner, you can reach back and help along another suffering, stressed-out person who needs to hear the good news that she can be a winner, too!

When things go bad, cheer up. Remember, they could always be worse. And, of course, if they do get worse, it will make your heart smile to remember that when it's this bad, it has to get better soon.

January 26

How I rejoice in the Lord! How he has blessed me!
(1 SAMUEL 2:1 TLB)

For so many of us, grief sweeps through our brains like a whirlwind, wiping out all sorts of brilliant ideas, not to mention the mundane facts we need to survive everyday life. Instead of criticizing yourself when you do something goofy, find a way to laugh about it. As someone said, if you find yourself tottering down the road to the Home for the Bewildered, you might as well enjoy the trip. Here are some suggestions for "living dangerously" when you're caught up in the crazies:

- Break out dancing every now and then—tap, rap, or jig. It'll help you pass the time until the men in the white coats come to take you away.

- Have chocolate pie for breakfast.

- Do not come in out of the rain.

- Pop popcorn without putting the lid on.

- Rip those tags off your new pillows!

- Wear two shoes that really don't match.

- Brush your teeth with Cheez Whiz.

Did you ever stop to think . . . and forget to start up again?

Here on earth you will have many trials and sorrows; but cheer up, for I have overcome the world. (JOHN 16:33 TLB)

Life is an adventure. Hang on to your hat and scream for all you're worth!

Real friends are those who, when you've made a fool of yourself, don't think you've done a permanent job.

There is more hope for a fool than for a man of quick temper. (PROVERBS 29:20 TLB)

Even when we're trapped in impossible predicaments, we can choose to laugh. Sure, being a joyful woman can sometimes be a challenge. But it's like that little message someone imagined coming from God:

I didn't say it would be easy.
I said it would be worth it!

What I'd really like to do when the plane is late or the luggage is lost is get upset—start whining and moaning. Or I want to be mad—raise my voice, harden my heart, tighten up my face, and unload a sharp tongue-lashing to any unfortunate soul who happens to cross my path. But frankly, I've tried those choices, and neither one is satisfying. As quickly as I vent my frustration I regret my thoughtless words and harsh remarks.

On the other hand, I can't remember *ever* regretting a kind word I somehow managed to share in tense times. Or a smile when I really wanted to scowl. Or a giggle instead of a complaint.

Light travels faster than sound. This is why some people appear bright until you hear them speak.

January 28

*I have leaned on you since the day I was born; you
have been my God since my mother gave me birth.*
(PSALM 22:10 NCV)

If we survive the high blood pressure and accelerated heart rates, the memories of parent-and-teenager driving sessions can be funny, if not especially soothing. In my case, the memory of teaching our son Tim to drive has become a cherished frozen picture in my mental scrapbook. We went to a nearby cemetery so Tim could learn how to negotiate the curving roadway that wound through the grounds. The speed limit was fifteen miles per hour, and there were rarely any other cars we could bump into. Still, there were a few screeching brakes and some wandering off the pavement. Now I laugh at those memories, and I'm so grateful for them when I go to that same cemetery . . . to visit Tim's grave.

My nerves are a-twitter; my hair has gone white.
My knees, they are knocking; I'm quaking with fright.
My whole life is streaking in front of my eyes.
"Dear Lord, please be with me!" I urgently cry.
My heart's in my throat, but at least I'm alive.
The problem? I'm teaching my son how to drive!

—ANN LUNA

When Joshua was very old, the LORD said to him,
"Joshua, you have grown old, but there is still much
land for you to take." (JOSHUA 13:1 NCV)

After my book *Living Somewhere Between Estrogen and Death* was published, I was inundated with stories and letters from women who wanted to tell me how the book helped them laugh while they wrestled with the most heartbreaking experiences life could throw at them. One of my favorite stories came from a woman in Chicago. She said she and her sister had brought along a copy of *Estrogen* when their eighty-year-old mother was hospitalized for her final illness. Sitting in their mother's hospital room, they took turns reading the book aloud to her. She said, "Barb, I'll always be grateful to you for that cherished image: my mother, *laughing*, on her deathbed!"

"Oh," I answered softly, "when did she die?"

"She *didn't* die—she lived!" the woman said, laughing heartily. "That was a year ago. She's fine now. We think it was all that *Estrogen* we read to her and all that laughing!"

Everyone has a photographic memory. But some folks don't have film.

January 30

The LORD, the God of Israel, has granted rest to his people. (1 CHRONICLES 23:25)

I'm all for being good to others. As we refresh others, we ourselves are refreshed (Proverbs 11:25). But Jesus taught us by example to get out of the rat race sometimes and recharge our batteries.

Jesus took time to enjoy Himself with others. He could have spent twenty-four hours a day healing the sick or teaching the multitudes, but you never see Jesus being pressured or stressed. The idea that you should never take time for yourself isn't biblical. In fact, it's a good way to disintegrate.

When frustrations develop into problems to stress you out, the best way to cope is to stop, catch your breath, and do something nice for yourself, not out of selfishness, but out of wisdom. All of us need our batteries recharged, probably a lot more often than we want to admit.

You can't turn back the clock, but you can wind it up again!

All things are possible for the one who believes.
(MARK 9:23 NCV)

When our son Larry was estranged from us and refused to contact us for many months, my fires of hope burned so low that one day I thought they had gone out. I drove up a viaduct near Disneyland, fully intending to drive over the edge and take my own life. Just as I reached the top, however, I began wondering if the fall to another freeway below would do the whole job. Perhaps I'd just be maimed and wind up making baskets in the Home for the Bewildered. I couldn't do it.

All hope was gone. That's when I told the Lord I just couldn't go on any longer. I just couldn't carry the burden of our son one more day. I gave Larry to Him. I *relinquished* him. An incredible change came over me almost instantaneously as I whispered the two words that have become a motto I now live by daily:

Whatever, Lord!

February 1

I may speak in different languages of people or even angels. But if I do not have love, I am only a noisy bell or a crashing cymbal. I may have the gift of prophecy. I may understand all the secret things of God and have all knowledge, and I may have faith so great I can move mountains. But even with all these things, if I do not have love, then I am nothing. I may give away everything I have, and I may even give my body as an offering to be burned. But I gain nothing if I do not have love.

Love is patient and kind. Love is not jealous, it does not brag, and it is not proud.

Love is not rude, is not selfish, and does not get upset with others. Love does not count up wrongs that have been done. Love is not happy with evil but is happy with the truth.

Love patiently accepts all things. It always trusts, always hopes, and always remains strong.

Love never ends. (1 CORINTHIANS 13:1–8 NCV)

February is the month of love. And nowhere is love defined more beautifully than in the Bible. To celebrate the beginning of a new month, read aloud this beautiful passage from 1 Corinthians to someone you love.

For God has not given us a spirit of fear, but of power and of love and of a sound mind. (2 TIMOTHY 1:7 NKJV)

Groundhog Day is a goofy tradition, isn't it? Whatever made us think a subterranean rodent could know anything about the next six weeks of weather? Nonetheless, the news cameras focus on the furry critter every February 2 to see whether he sees his shadow, darts back into his hole, and thus dooms the entire nation to another six weeks of winter.

While we're observing goofy customs, we might as well share a few laughs. Here are some of my favorites for a February morning:

There are three ways to get something done:
1. Do it yourself.
2. Hire someone to do it for you.
3. Forbid your kids to do it.

* * *

WARNING! I KNOW KARATE!
(and three other Chinese words)

* * *

If you have your feet firmly on the ground and your head in the clouds . . . you're walking in a fog.
—SHERRY WEAVER

February 3

Now you are sad, but I will see you again and you will be happy, and no one will take away your joy.
(JOHN 16:22 NCV)

R ecently I saw a church sign that said:

"INTERESTED IN GOING TO HEAVEN?
APPLY HERE FOR FLIGHT TRAINING!"

That's us! Soon we'll be putting into practice what we've been trained to expect. I like to call this training "Rapture practice." I think we should go out in the backyard and practice for the Rapture, that time when we will meet Jesus in the air as He returns. I said this once at a meeting, and a lady asked me, "When you do your Rapture practice, do you do it on the ground or on a trampoline?"

No matter where we are when it happens, one of these days, He's gonna TOOT and we're gonna SCOOT right outta here. And I can hardly wait!

Life is hard, then you die . . .
And get to be in heaven!

Be sure of this—that I am with you always, even to the end of the world. (MATTHEW 28:20 TLB)

Jesus knows how you feel when you're hurt, scared, or alone. He knows what it's like to suffer; He suffered on our behalf! And He also knows what it's like, late at night, to feel such heartache you think you'll die. On the night before He was crucified, he led His disciples to Gethsemane and told them, "My soul is overwhelmed with sorrow to the point of death." And certainly He knows what it's like to feel all alone, because those same disciples—His closest friends and followers—suddenly disappeared when the bad times started.

Darcey Hripak

Jesus understands. And He's always with you to wrap you in His comfort blanket of love.

You are tuned to radio station W-H-Y, broadcasting continuously, twenty-four hours a day, from somewhere within your head.

February 5

"No one can hide where I cannot see him," says the
LORD. (JEREMIAH 23:24 NCV)

My pregnancies occurred back in the Dark Ages when obstetricians tried to strictly limit their patients' weight gain to only fifteen pounds or so. It was a real problem for me, because my fat cells apparently absorb calories from fumes—I don't even have to swallow! Luckily, on my first appointment, I noticed that the doctor's scale was next to a window sill. So whenever I was weighed I would secretly put my finger down on the sill and PUSH . . . and it would make me seem to weigh four or five pounds less.

Then one day I was shocked to see they had painted the room and moved the scale to the middle of the floor, away from the window sill! When the nurse weighed me it looked as if I had gained ten pounds in only a couple of weeks! The doctor threw such a fit that I finally had to confess.

My sins always find me out. But even when they do . . .
God loves me so much that He will accept me just as I am
. . . But He loves me too much to leave me that way!

We who have run for our very lives to God have every reason to grab the promised hope with both hands and never let go. It's an unbreakable spiritual lifeline, reaching past all appearances right to the very presence of God. (HEBREWS 6:18–19 TM)

Bruce Larson tells a story about a man who was taking a cruise on an ocean liner. Somehow one of his socks got away from him and blew over the railing, forever lost. Without a thought, the man flipped the other sock over the railing too. He knew when he was looking at a hopeless situation.

In contrast, many of us would take the remaining sock home and KEEP it, hoping a mate might miraculously turn up sometime. But all we would be doing is cluttering up our sock drawer. Instead, like the man on the ship, we need to let go of the painful situations that are out of our control and step out, unencumbered, knowing God holds our future in His hands.

You can't have everything. Where would you put it?

Oh, the joys of those who put their trust in him!
(PSALM 2:12 TLB)

In her book, *Riches Stored in Secret Places*, Verdell Davis talks about moving through grief one slow step at a time. She describes the monasteries of ancient Europe where "the monks walked the dark hallways with candles secured to the toes of their shoes, giving light only for the next step." Eventually she came "to grasp the meaning of light for the next step—as [the monks] walked, the light always went just before them."

Even while she wondered why God "could not light the way a little more brightly when we are so consumed with pain and fear," she learned that in her journey through grief, "the candle on the toe of each shoe is really enough. Because God Himself is the candle."

In the darkest pit of despair, when God gives us the light to take only one step at a time, His message to us is still simply:

Trust Me.

*If you treat every situation as a life-and-death matter . . .
you will die a lot.*

*Take a new grip with your tired hands, stand firm on
your shaky legs, and mark out a straight, smooth path for
your feet so that those who follow you, though weak and
lame, will not fall and hurt themselves, but become
strong.* (HEBREWS 12:12–13 TLB)

We need to put things into eternal perspective
and remember the promise of Romans 8:28
that God makes *everything*—even calamities—work for
our good. Sometimes it's awfully hard to wait for the
"good" to "work." And every now and then, when we
feel as if we're plunging to ever-greater depths, we
can't help but wonder if anything good will really
come out of our misery. A stressed-out woman agreed.
She said:

> I know these trials are supposed to make me strong—
> but I'm not sure I WANT to be SAMSON!

Just remember, no matter how far you plummet . . .

> The Lord lifts the fallen
> and those bent beneath their loads.
> (PSALM 145:14 TLB)

*If all else fails to boost your spirits—find something to
laugh about!*

February 9

Those who hope in the LORD will renew their strength.
They will soar on wings like eagles; they will run and
not grow weary, they will walk and not be faint.
(ISAIAH 40:31)

When people around us are rejoicing and praising God while we are struggling through deep mire and floodwaters, we begin to wonder if something is wrong with us. We begin to feel like second-class Christians. And then the final straw comes if these people who are being blessed and who don't face the problems we do are quick to give us the glib answers: "Just praise the Lord . . . You are just not praising the Lord enough . . . What you need to do is take your stand . . . Just praise the Lord!"

When the floodwaters of the cesspool have come up to your very soul, you don't need challenges; you need COMFORT. You need a friend to come alongside and say, "I am hurting with you . . . I am standing with you . . . I am weeping with you. I am undergirding you as best I can. Link your shield of faith with mine and somehow we will make it together."

Please spare me the ghastly details of your happiness!

The way of the LORD is a refuge for the righteous.
(PROVERBS 10:29)

If you are interested in the hereafter, remember that the HERE determines the AFTER!

February 11

I pray that the God who gives hope will fill you with much joy and peace while you trust in him. Then your hope will overflow by the power of the Holy Spirit. (ROMANS 15:13 NCV)

Even when we've landed with our faces in the dust, even when we are caught in a wringer, we can always have hope. And even when hope is lost, it can be regained; we can refocus our perspective. As we wait on the Lord, our strength will be renewed, and so will our joy. In the Scriptures, hope and joy often go together. I like to say hope and joy are sisters.

Hope is God's sustaining power that creates a consistent flow of joy deep beneath the waves of trouble and the winds of sorrow. Hope infuses the mind and heart with joy and gives us the deep confidence that we are God's forgiven children and that He will never let us go.

The surest mark of a Christian is not faith or love but JOY.

And if a house be divided against itself, that house cannot stand. (MARK 3:25 KJV)

Abraham Lincoln said, "Most folks are as happy as they make up their minds to be." So today, in honor of Old Abe on his birthday, let's make up our minds to be happy. Here are some funnies to help you laugh.

Practical Guide for Successful Living:
Put your head under the pillow and scream.

* * *

When your dreams turn to dust . . . vacuum!

* * *

Money isn't everything,
but it sure keeps the kids in touch!

* * *

Change is inevitable—except from a vending machine.

* * *

The things that come to those who wait may be the things left by those who got there first.

* * *

We're all in this together.
You're just in a little deeper.

February 13

Love each other as I have loved you. (JOHN 15:12 NCV)

At the coffee shop where Bill and I often go for lunch, the owner's wife, Joyce, brought about forty scraps of paper to me, asking if I could help her prepare a Valentine's Day surprise for her husband, Bob. The little papers contained all the little love poems Bob had written to her over the years. He had no idea that she had saved them all. Joyce asked us to help her get them printed up so she could give them to Bob in a little booklet.

We had them typeset. Our daughter-in-love Shannon designed a clever cover, and we compiled the poems into bright red folders. When the big day came, Joyce called Bob over to our table and handed him a red folder. Bob stood there in his white chef's hat, amazed to see all those poems! He had tears in his eyes to realize Joyce had treasured his loving words for all those years. It was a wonderful Valentine's Day for all of us: HER love and HIS poems—but WE were blessed by it, too!

There is a chord in every heart that has a sigh in it if you use the right touch.

So these three things continue forever: faith, hope,
and love. And the greatest of these is love.
(1 CORINTHIANS 13:13 NCV)

On Valentine's Day a wrinkled old man sat on the bus seat holding a bunch of fresh roses. Across the aisle was a young girl whose sad eyes seemed to be locked on the floor—except for moments when she glanced back again and again at the man's flowers.

The time came for the old man to get off. Impulsively he thrust the flowers into the girl's lap. "I can see you love the roses," he explained. "I was taking them to my wife, but I know she would like for you to have them. I'll tell her I gave them to you."

The girl accepted the flowers with a delighted smile then watched the old man get off the bus . . . and walk through the gates of a cemetery.

It doesn't take great wisdom to energize a person, but it does take sixty seconds. That's the amount of time it takes to walk over and gently hold someone we love.

—GARY SMALLEY

February 15

Words come again and again to our ears, but we never hear enough, nor can we ever really see all we want to see. (ECCLESIASTES 1:8 NCV)

"What I said was, 'I'm feeling *rheumatic!*'"

Love sees through a telescope, not a microscope.

May the Lord bless and protect you; may the Lord's face radiate with joy because of you; may he be gracious to you, show you his favor, and give you his peace.
(NUMBERS 6:24–26 TLB)

It's fun to collect funny sayings and improper uses of words, sometimes called *malapropisms*. Here's a fun-filled list someone sent to me:

- If you can't do it right, do it yourself.
- No news travels fast.
- Every clown has a silver lining.
- Run it up the flagpole and see who sits on it.
- Am I my brother's beeper?
- No man can serve two masters with one stone.
- Rome wasn't burned in a day.
- It's on the fork of my tongue.
- People who live in glass houses shouldn't throw sour grapes.

What's so remarkable about love at first sight? It's when people have been looking at each other for years that it becomes remarkable!

A cheerful heart is good medicine. (PROVERBS 17:22)

Laughter is not only good for the body, it's good for the soul. Psychologically, the ability to see humor in a situation is as important as the laughter itself. A sense of humor can help you overlook the unattractive, tolerate the unpleasant, cope with the unexpected, and smile through the unbearable. A genuine sense of humor is the pole that adds balance to our steps as we walk the tightrope of life. And if we happen to fall into one of life's inevitable cesspools, a healthy sense of humor can help us splash our way to shore. I like the wisdom that says:

OUR FIVE SENSES ARE INCOMPLETE
WITHOUT THE SIXTH—A SENSE OF HUMOR.

Having a sense of humor doesn't mean you go around laughing at everything. A person with a sense of humor doesn't make jokes out of life; she only sees the funny stuff that's already there. In other words, she can see the silly side along with the serious side.

Laughter is the hand of God on the shoulder of a troubled world.

We also have joy with our troubles, because we know that these troubles produce patience. And patience produces character, and character produces hope. (ROMANS 5:3–4 NCV)

Who of us has not watched tensions dissolve in the presence of love and humor? We see this happen continually in our Spatula meetings. Deep pain is present. Depressing stories abound. But then somebody will say something humorous, and it will pick up everyone's mood.

For example, at a recent Spatula meeting, a grief-stricken father said his son had decided to become a girl. He was planning to have dinner with his son, who had already warned him he was coming "in drag." All fifty people in the room were silent. Suddenly I suggested, "Maybe you could wear your wife's clothes and your son would feel more comfortable."

There was a moment of stunned silence. Then somebody laughed, and pretty soon everyone was laughing, including the father. Humor had stepped in to save the situation when good, practical advice was, well, impractical.

An optimist laughs to forget. A pessimist forgets to laugh.

Everything that goes into a life of pleasing God has been miraculously given to us. . . . We were also given absolutely terrific promises to pass on to you—your tickets to participation in the life of God. (2 PETER 1:3–4 TM)

Sad events in our lives here on earth make us long for that day in the "sweet by and by" when we'll "meet on that beautiful shore," as the beautiful old hymn describes heaven. The hope of heaven sustains us in our earthly struggles and pushes us closer to God. As Joni Eareckson Tada said:

Suffering hurries the heart homeward.

For Christians, *home* is *heaven!* That's our eternal home as well as our enduring hope, a hope someone defined as:

> **H**e
> **O**ffers
> **P**eace
> **E**ternal.

The knowledge that we'll someday enjoy "peace eternal" means we can face *anything* here on earth as long as we focus on the joy that's waiting for us in heaven.

Bumper Snicker: *Rapture Ready!*

*Love each other like brothers and sisters. Give each
other more honor than you want for yourselves.*
(ROMANS 12:10 NCV)

My husband and I are very different people.
When we got married I intuitively knew I
needed someone like Bill to balance my own tendency
to be too excited, all helter-skelter and disorganized.
And I think Bill sensed he needed me to offset his tendency to take life too seriously. So we got married and
learned that, while opposites attract, they also must
adjust to each other.

I'll never expect Bill to be as happy and bubbling
with enthusiasm as I am, and he has finally decided I'll
never be as orderly, methodical, and organized as he is.
For example, the other day he got a new key ring and
spent almost an hour putting on all the keys so they
would all face the "right" way. He says he can't use my
key ring because I have them jumbled every which way.

(And this is good, because I usually can't *find* my
keys anyway!)

**The best exercise for good relationships is bending over
backward.**

When we have the opportunity to help anyone, we should do it. (GALATIANS 6:10 NCV)

Opportunities come in all shapes and sizes. What if those things you see now as *stumbling* blocks could be seen instead as *building* blocks? Think of them as bricks—and remember that bricks can build *walls* or *walkways*. You can follow the yellow brick road to where you want to be, or you can remain stymied by that big wall that seals off any progress you want to make. It all depends on how you look at those blocks and bricks!

Changing our perspective calls for a willingness to see things differently. That's the key to developing a positive attitude regardless of what happens to us. I saw an example of that after Southern California was devastated by one of the most extensive wildfires in history. One of the hardest-hit areas was Laguna Beach, but one man whose house had burned to the ground kept a positive attitude. He said:

I'm looking at the bright side. I finally got ride of those darn termites!

Jesus turns the Valley of Despair into a Door of Hope.

*People don't hide a light under a bowl. They put it on a
lampstand so the light shines for all the people in the
house. In the same way, you should be a light for other
people. Live so that they will see the good things you do
and will praise your Father in heaven.*
(MATTHEW 5:15–16 NCV)

One of my favorite childhood memories is of
walking home at night, strolling along the
snowy sidewalks, and spotting my house from quite a
way off. Light was streaming out the windows, making the snow glisten on our front lawn like transient
diamonds scattered over the ground.

Now I'm nearer my *heavenly* home than my childhood home. And we know that the light pouring out of
heaven, extending a warm welcome to all those who
love the Lord, is God Himself. He is the *real* reason
why heaven will be so wonderful. As fabulous as
they'll be, our mansions will be just dwelling places.
The angelic choir, the streets of gold, the pearly gates,
and all those other beautiful images in paradise will
just be window dressing.

*Jesus was born in a stable so that we may have a man-
sion when we die.*

Kind mercy wins over harsh judgment every time.
(JAMES 2:13 TM)

We like to say that Spatula Ministries uses a spatula of love to scrape parents down when something about their children has caused them to land on the ceiling. AIDS, addictions, prostitution, cults, and all sorts of other problems cause many folks, even Christians, to reject these adult children and heap scorn upon them—and sometimes upon their parents too. That's why I loved the postscript a friend added to her letter:

> Barbara, keep doing what you do. There are churches and Christian programs around the world that minister to the ninety-and-nine. But you are reaching out to that one lost sheep.

My friend's encouragement reminded me that it might be *my* arms reaching out to that "one lost sheep," but it's *God's* love flowing through me that accomplishes the healing. As someone said:

Broken skin heals in days . . . broken bones in weeks or months . . . broken hearts and spirits sometimes in years . . . broken souls heal only by God's grace.

Christ gave gifts to people—he made some to be apostles, some to be prophets, some to go and tell the Good News, and some to have the work of caring for and teaching God's people. (EPHESIANS 4:11 NCV)

Priceless Gifts to Give for Free

The gift of listening: No interrupting, no daydreaming, no planning your responses. Just listen.

The gift of affection: Be generous with appropriate hugs, kisses, pats on the back, and handholding.

The gift of laughter: Share articles, funny stories, and cartoons to tell someone, "I love to laugh with you."

The gift of a compliment: A simple and sincere "You look great in red," "You did a super job," or "That was a wonderful meal" can make someone's day.

The gift of solitude: Be sensitive to the times when others want nothing more than to be left alone.

The gift of a cheerful disposition: The easiest way to feel good is to extend a kind word to someone, even if it's just saying hello or thank you.

The gift of a prayer: Let your friends and loved ones know you pray for them—then do it!

February 25

The right word spoken at the right time is as beautiful as gold apples in a silver bowl. (PROVERBS 25:11 NCV)

There are so many ways we can follow Jesus' example and be a servant to others—sometimes simply by doing ordinary work with cheerfulness. A friend's letter reminded me of that fact. She wrote to say that her uncle, a Christian, went with his wife to a Hardee's drive-through and ordered breakfast. The couple ate there often, she said, and the boy who took their order recognized her uncle's voice and said, "Come on up, partner. We're waiting for you."

Just then the uncle grabbed his chest and said to his wife, "I'll see you in heaven!" And he was gone. The woman wrote:

At my uncle's funeral the minister said, "The voice over the speaker may have been the order-taker's, but it was a message straight from Jesus: 'Come on up, partner; we're waiting for you.'"

If you thought your words would be the last earthly thing someone heard, would it make a difference in what you said and how you said it?

The blue of heaven is bigger than the clouds.

There is not a single man in all the earth who is always good and never sins. (ECCLESIASTES 7:20 TLB)

Erma Bombeck was right when she said, "Guilt is the gift that keeps on giving." When our son Steve was killed in Vietnam, I blamed myself for allowing him to enlist early in the marine corps. When our oldest son, Tim, died in a car crash driving home from Alaska, I thought, *Why didn't I insist that he ship his car by boat and FLY home?* And when our homosexual son, Larry, disappeared for eleven years, I was convinced my words had driven him away.

Guilt tortures us with its own special kind of misery. But no matter WHAT we have done—whether or not we somehow caused the current catastrophe—Jesus died to erase it from our slates. It's GONE! God cleanses us and makes us new. The one thing God CANNOT see is our sin because it is covered by the blood of Jesus. We are forgiven! Hallelujah!

Worry doesn't help tomorrow's troubles, but it does ruin today's happiness.

February 27

He will have no fear of bad news; his heart is steadfast, trusting in the LORD. (PSALM 112:7)

INSTRUCTIONS:
As bad news approaches,
flash this sign.

Today is the tomorrow you worried about yesterday—
but not nearly enough.

Call upon me in the day of trouble; I will deliver you.
(PSALM 50:15)

While many parents have a hint of foreboding when bad news is about to be dumped on them, for others it's a bolt out of the blue. I've received a lot of late-night "911" calls from these desperate parents. One distraught mother called me from an airplane. Her son and his girlfriend had driven her to the airport, and as she got out of the car, she said to him, "I'm so glad you have such a nice girlfriend."

Her son turned to her and said, "Mom, it's time I told you. She's not my girlfriend. She's into girls, and I'm into guys." And with that he set her bags on the sidewalk, gave her a hug, and drove off!

We all have seen dreams turn to ashes—ugly things, hopeless experiences—but beauty for ashes is God's exchange. In the midst of the darkness you will learn lessons you might never have learned in the day. Offer yourself to God and ask for a spirit of praise so your whole being will be restored.

When things get rough, remember: It's the rubbing that brings out the shine.

February 29

There is a right time for everything: . . . A time to cry;
A time to laugh. (ECCLESIASTES 3:1, 4 TLB)

A friend who went to bed for a year "to count the dots on the ceiling and wish my mind had an off switch so that I could stop feeling so crazy all the time" said she finally came to a crucial understanding:

> Call me a slow learner if you will, but after years of counseling and a better understanding of God's grace in my life, I am finally beginning to understand what it means to take care of myself in the midst of life's cesspools. . . . I'm doing a better job of letting go of those people and situations I can't control. I never cease to be amazed at the peace and joy that floods my life these days as a result of changing what I CAN change: MY ATTITUDE!

Beautiful flowers can grow on dung hills.

I saw myself so stupid and so ignorant. . . . But even so,
you love me! You are holding my right hand!
(PSALM 73:22–23 TLB)

Once when I was invited to hold a two-day conference in my childhood church in Michigan,
some generous folks loaned my sister, Janet, and me a
lovely new car to use while I was there. At least twice
while using the car, we stopped to ask for directions
and couldn't figure out how to get the car window
open. Instead we had to open the door to talk to people
on the street. We couldn't find the window-opener but-
ton. We pushed all the buttons on the dashboard but
only succeeded in turning on the radio, wipers, and air
conditioner. When we returned the car, I thanked the
owner and said, "This is a beautiful car, but how do
you get the windows down?"

His eyes widened as he pointed to a handle on the
door and said, "You just turn the crank."

Crank? Janet and I looked at the door, and there it
was—the "old-fashioned" crank handle that *all* cars
used to have a few years ago.

If you can't laugh at yourself . . . I'll be glad to do it for
you.

March 2

The LORD your God will bless you in all your harvest and in all the work of your hands, and your joy will be complete. (DEUTERONOMY 16:15)

When you're in pain because of a loss or because someone is driving you into the Home for the Bewildered, you think you will never be normal again. A heavy mantle of grief may enclose you in the thick fog of despair, but tears, talking, and time will work wonders. One morning you will wake up and realize suddenly that you're not thinking about your pain. You will actually be able to hear the birds sing or see a fluffy white cloud drift across the sky. On that day you will have a glimmer of hope and begin to realize there is something more to life than your specific problem. To put it another way, the night of grief will end, and, as Psalm 30:5 (NCV) promises:

JOY COMES IN THE MORNING.

The intense pain will ease up, flatten out, and not be so encompassing. Scar tissue may remain from the hurt you suffer, but your deep wounds will heal.

When someone says, "Life is hard," ask him, "Compared with what?"

And the Word was made flesh, and dwelt among us, (and we beheld his glory, the glory as of the only begotten of the Father,) full of grace and truth. (JOHN 1:14 KJV)

race is mentioned 170 times in the King James Version of the Bible, beginning with "Noah found grace in the eyes of the LORD" (Genesis 6:8 KJV). Jesus never used the word *grace*. God left that for Paul and the apostles, but if you want to describe grace in one word, it is *Jesus*.

Grace (Jesus) is the answer for our guilt and failure.

Grace (Jesus) is the strength we need to cope with life.

Grace (Jesus) is the promise that gives us the hope that keeps us going.

> **God's**
> **Riches**
> **At**
> **Christ's**
> **Expense**

The soul would have no rainbows if the eyes had no tears.

March 4

God's lamp shined on my head, and I walked through darkness by his light. (JOB 29:3 NCV)

When you have life's pressures under control, you're like a pigeon that soars high above the problems. But when life drops a load of stress on you, you're more like the statue, all covered with pigeon poop!

When that happens, there are three basic responses you can make:

- You can be as stoic as a statue.
- You can throw a pity party, complaining loudly that life is for the birds.
- You can accept what's happening and maintain a positive attitude at the same time.

When you're able to take your bloopers, boo-boos, and blunders and see the humor in the situation, you reduce your stress and turn it into a positive force that will help you grow and WIN.

There are two approaches to the future: anxiety and optimism. One will make you dread tomorrow; the other will help you welcome it.

Be glad that you are his; let those who seek the LORD be happy. (1 CHRONICLES 16:10 NCV)

Humor is a powerful force, and anything that makes us laugh in the face of life's adversity is valuable. A good motto is:

> Love makes the world go 'round,
> but laughter keeps you from getting dizzy.

So, that's what I try to share in my books and my talks around the country—plenty of smiles, chuckles, and laughs. Of course, there is a purpose to my zaniness—to encourage you wherever you are as you experience life's ongoing trials. When you find yourself trapped in a dark tunnel of despair, wrap yourself in His comfort blanket and remember that nothing can separate you from the love of God. He has brought you this far, and He will NEVER leave you. You WILL survive, and you WILL find the light at the end of the tunnel. Then one day you will look back and see how God used your painful situations to fine-tune you for His glory, making you a golden treasure in His sight.

The best thing about the future is that it comes one day at a time.

March 6

His miracles are unforgettable. The LORD is kind and merciful. He gives food to those who fear him. He remembers his agreement forever. (PSALM 111:4–5 NCV)

Laughter is nutrition for your soul, a tourniquet to stop the bleeding of a broken heart, an encouraging tonic for the discouraged. We need to laugh for our physical, emotional, and spiritual health.

Sometimes folks say my specialty is making people laugh, but that's not really my major goal. I use laughter to flatten out the pain folks feel because of the blows life has dealt them. Remember: Life is full of bumps, potholes, and even washed-out bridges, and . . .

HUMOR IS TO LIFE AS
SHOCK ABSORBERS ARE TO AUTOMOBILES.

Laughter is like premium gasoline: *It helps take the knock out of living!*

Moses didn't realize as he came back down the mountain with the tablets that his face glowed from being in the presence of God. (EXODUS 34:29 TLB)

All things considered, you can see why I could use a good laugh.

God can help you find the Sonshine inside yourself so you can laugh again. No matter where you are, He is with you.

March 8

Don't be afraid! Stand still and you will see the Lord save you today. (EXODUS 14:13 NCV)

ear Barbara,

Lately I have had several fears that I may be going off my rocker. How can I know if this is what is happening to me?

Fearful in Fayetteville

Dear Fearful,

We know that one out of every four people in this country is mentally unbalanced. So, you just think of your three closest friends . . . If they seem to be okay, then you're the one!

God can use reversals to move us forward.

Moses' arms finally became too tired to hold up the rod any longer, so Aaron and Hur rolled a stone for him to sit on, and they stood on each side, holding up his hands until sunset. As a result, Joshua and his troops crushed the army of Amalek. (EXODUS 17:12–13 TLB)

Those of us who've heard heartbreaking pronouncements—"Mom and Dad, I'm gay." "I'm on drugs." "I'm so sorry, Mr. and Mrs. Smith. Your son . . . I'm so sorry."—can't help but laugh now at the things that *used* to send us into orbit: "Like my hair, Mom? It's 'napalm green.'" "I'm getting an F in English." "I dented the fender." "I lost your credit card."

Yes, we've been through the wringer, walked through the fire, crawled through the tunnel. But in the trials we've faced, something good has happened too: God has fine-tuned us so we are more compassionate, more caring, more loving, more aware of others' pain. We have credentials for sharing. And just by walking, talking, and breathing, we encourage others whose journey through grief is just beginning that they, too, can survive.

A sense of humor is like a needle and thread: *It will patch up so many things.*

March 10

Gates, open all the way. Open wide, aged doors so the glorious King will come in. (PSALM 24:7 NCV)

I don't really like being around old people—so it's a little tough realizing that *now I AM one!* It's easy for me to slip into the mind-set that portrays most old people as befuddled senior citizens: endlessly forgetful, hopelessly confused, and, in general, a pain to be around. When that image comes to mind, I can't help but whisper a prayer, begging, "*Please, please, PLEASE, Lord! Don't ever let me be old!*"

But the only way to avoid getting old is to die young, and that just wasn't God's plan for me. Old age happens to us without any effort at all on our parts. We blow out the candles on our twenty-first birthday cake, and *poof!* The next thing we know, we're wearing goofy party hats and singing "Auld Lang Syne" in some retirement home in Florida and wondering, *How did this happen?*

I've reached the age where it's harder to think of my body as a temple. It's more like a building project that got out of control!

The secret things belong to the LORD. (DEUTERONOMY 29:29)

The radio call-in show was going well, and I had fielded several easy questions. Then a caller frantically reeled off an incredible barrage of problems: Her husband was alcoholic. Her son was gay, her unmarried daughter was pregnant, and her house had burned down. The talk-show host and I looked at each other in bewilderment. What could she do? Where could she go? The pause grew into a pregnant silence. The host fidgeted as I frantically searched my mind for something that might help this poor woman. Finally I blurted out, "God only knows!"

There was a moment of shocked silence, then people in the studio audience started tittering. The host started chuckling, and then even the woman on the other end of the line began to laugh as she realized that my seemingly flippant answer was true. That's why I love Deuteronomy 29:29. When we are at wit's-end corner, when life is a mystery that seems to have no answer—*only God knows* the answers.

Humor is the prelude to faith, and laughter is the beginning of prayer. —REINHOLD NIEBUHR

March 12

I am like an olive tree growing in God's Temple. I trust God's love forever and ever. (PSALM 52:8 NCV)

One of the most creative ways to forgive I've ever seen came from a woman who wrote to me:

I have strengthened my prayer life by weeding my flowerbed. I used to have names on all the weeds and really would hoe, chop, and mutilate people who had frustrated me. Now my weeds are still named, but instead of chopping them, I gently pull them and pause and pray for them. I call it the love approach instead of the angry approach. I also have added to my list those who need extra encouragement through prayer and not just my "hit list."

Cheer up! Get to your feet. Jesus is calling you.
(MARK 10:49 NCV)

Not long ago I began noticing how the household products I use affect my attitude. For example, I like to wash my dishes in JOY detergent because it reminds me that joy is the land of beginning again for every Christian. Happiness depends on what is going on around us, but joy bubbles up from deep within because of what God does for us. Happiness is elusive and can be wiped out in a second, but abiding joy from the Lord is like a deep river down in our hearts that just keeps flowing.

Seeing that big bottle of JOY by my sink every day encourages me to look for other products with names that affect my attitude. That's how I've managed to stock my cupboard—and my attitude—with ZEST, CHEER, GLAD, SPARKLE, and a host of other reminders to smile and be happy as I rid my home of dirt, grime, rust, and stains.

This is a test. It is only a test. If this were your actual life, you would have been given better instructions.

March 14

As a deer thirsts for streams of water, so I thirst for you, God. I thirst for the living God. (Psalm 42:1–2 NCV)

Laughing together over life's little twists and turns is a great way to let off steam and keep stress at a minimum. A story I tell on myself occurred while I was speaking in a church. I asked that some water be left on the podium, and sure enough, when I got up to speak, there was a lovely embossed chalice full of water.

As I spoke I kept sipping from the goblet, and by the time I finished, ALL the water was gone. Later, the conference hostess came up and apologized because she had forgotten to put the drinking water on the podium. She told me I had been drinking from a chalice of holy water the pastor used to baptize babies! At that point I had a choice: decide to be ill or decide it was funny. You can guess which choice I made: I laughed.

When you're willing to tell funny little personal stories on yourself, you'll have all kinds of fun. As someone said:

The shortest distance between two people is a smile.

The LORD is in his holy temple; the LORD sits on his throne in heaven. He sees what people do; he keeps his eye on them. (PSALM 11:4 NCV)

Maybe it's just a hormone thing, but lately, thoughts of heaven have completely absorbed me. It's become a joyous preoccupation for me to consider the wonderful life awaiting us there. Thoughts of heaven give us *encouragement* as we struggle through difficulties, *renewal* when we find ourselves sinking in the spiritual doldrums, and *laughter* when we think we'll never laugh again.

A friend once closed a letter to me with the quip, "Until He comes or I go!" The Rapture can't come soon enough for me! I'm ready! So if I sometimes seem a little distracted these days, it's not because of advancing age or approaching senility. It's because I keep one ear tuned toward heaven, listening for the sound of that trumpet announcing Jesus' return. On that day, He's gonna toot, and I'm gonna scoot!

Overheard at a senior citizens meeting: *"You know you're getting old when you make mental notes to yourself and then find you've misplaced them."*

March 16

I will not die, but live, and I will tell what the Lord has done. (PSALM 118:17 NCV)

Our son Barney was to meet Bill, my friend Lynda, and me at the train station in San Diego. Our train arrived right on time, but Barney wasn't there. We ended up huddled on a bench in the waiting area, alone except for a homeless man leaning against the wall. Long, straggly black hair hung out of his filthy baseball cap. His trousers, stained and torn, were about four sizes too big, and his shirt was ragged. Puffs of smoke arose from the cigarette dangling from his mouth.

He seemed to be watching us. When he slowly started ambling our way, Lynda hissed in my ear, "Barb! He's coming to rob us!" When the man was just a few feet away, I stiffened, preparing for the worst. Suddenly he spoke.

"Hi, Mom!"

MOM? It was Barney, playing a trick on us! He jerked off the cap with the fake hair, tossed away the fake cigarette, grabbed me in a sudden bear hug, and laughed until he was out of breath. Some days I think I *still* haven't recovered!

Learn from your parents' mistakes. Use birth control.

We know that in all things God works for the good of those who love him. (Romans 8:28)

When our son Tim was killed by a drunk driver, many wonderful Christian friends tried to be comforting, quoting Scriptures and urging me to zip up my anger and distress quickly. I believed the verses they were quoting, but the raw edges of my heart were still bleeding too much. I needed to grieve.

To escape, I would drive alone at night to a dump a few miles away. There I would sob and sometimes even scream. This was my way of venting emotions that HAD to be released. God doesn't say to grieve not; instead, His Word says, "that you may not grieve as others do who have no hope" (1 Thessalonians 4:13 RSV).

Now I can look back and see how Romans 8:28 *is* true. God *is* faithful, but the timing of my friends' reminders was all wrong. It is better to just put your arm around a grieving person and say, "I love you— God loves you." The simple truth is this:

When grief is the freshest, the words should be the fewest.

March 18

A happy heart makes the face cheerful. (PROVERBS 15:13)

According to my birth certificate, I am living somewhere between estrogen and death, or, as someone said, between menopause and LARGE PRINT! But I don't have to *act* my age because, thank God, I've discovered a wonderful antiaging remedy. It won't actually turn back the clock, and it's certainly not a new wonder drug. In fact, it's been promoted since biblical times as a cure for a wide variety of problems (see Proverbs 17:22). And it's no secret, either; lots of people use it. It's the same God-given gift that's kept me functioning through some heartbreaking tragedies.

What is it?

Laughter. A sense of humor. An attitude expressed by Oscar Wilde's motto: "Life is too important to be taken seriously." A tendency to look for joy throughout the journey, to find a way to laugh at *everything* life throws my way—even death. How could anyone laugh at death? Well, consider what the late Dorothy Parker suggested for the epitaph on her own tombstone: "Excuse my dust."

Don't worry about senility. . . . When it hits you, you won't know it. —BILL COSBY

Get to know the God of your fathers. Worship and serve him with a clean heart and a willing mind, for the Lord sees every heart and understands and knows every thought. If you seek him, you will find him.
(1 CHRONICLES 28:9 TLB)

Thanks for helping me over the hump!

Conceit may puff people up, but it never props them up.

March 20

Whatever is true, whatever is noble, whatever is right, whatever is pure, whatever is lovely, whatever is admirable—if anything is excellent or praiseworthy—think about such things. (PHILIPPIANS 4:8)

How we use the time God gives us is our choice every day. We can live as though Christ died yesterday, rose today, and is coming tomorrow, or we can live as though Christ died, period. We can count God-given gifts, or we can count calamities. We can count blessings, or we can count life's blows and burdens. It's our choice.

"But Barb," people ask me, "how can I choose to be positive when life is so negative?" Remember Philippians 4:8. You will be joyful if you want to think that way. Or you will be sad and depressed if you so choose. As someone said:

An optimist looks at an oyster
and expects to find a pearl.
A pessimist looks at an oyster
and expects ptomaine poisoning!

If you faithfully obey the commands I am giving you today—to love the LORD your God and to serve him with all your heart and with all your soul—then I will send rain on your land in its season, both autumn and spring rains, so that you may gather in your grain, new wine and oil. (DEUTERONOMY 11:13–14)

Happy first day of spring! Enjoy the spring showers that cleanse the air and help the flowers to grow. Let those showers remind you of one of my favorite verses:

She who waters others will also be watered herself.
(Proverbs 11:25 adapted)

March 22

Don't be sad, because the joy of the LORD will make you strong. (NEHEMIAH 8:10 NCV)

Maybe you think no one else has a problem as bad as yours. Maybe you think you're the only one who has lain awake at night wracked with the stomach-churning pain you're suffering. You think no one else has felt like an elephant was sitting on her chest. You can't believe anyone else has ever had an invisible shag rug stuck in her throat. Maybe you even think you're the only person whose teeth itched!

You're wrong.

All of us hurting parents have wrestled with that elephant, and even now I sometimes feel that shag rug creeping back up into my throat. My teeth haven't itched for a long time—but I'll never forget how it felt when they did! The important thing is to KEEP BREATHING . . . and KEEP BELIEVING! There is hope for all of us hurting parents, no matter how deeply mired in the mud we are.

When Jesus said, "In this world you will have trouble," . . . He wasn't kidding! (See John 16:33.)

A wife of noble character who can find? She is worth far more than rubies. . . . She is clothed with strength and dignity; she can laugh at the days to come.
(PROVERBS 31:10, 25)

Some folks tell me, "But Barbara, I'm not very good at laughing. Besides, I don't have a lot to laugh about right now."

I understand, but laughing is like a lot of things—if you want to be GOOD at it, you have to WORK at it. To start your day, try this simple exercise: Stand in front of the mirror, place your hands on your tummy, and laugh. It's okay if you can only manage one big "HA!" at first. Then try a big "HA HA!" Keep adding more "HA's" until you've got your diaphragm going, and before you know it, the laughter will be rolling out of you. This may sound a little crazy, but it works. You can literally jump-start yourself into having a good laugh just about any time you want to.

And remember:

**We don't laugh because we're happy;
we're happy because we laugh!**

March 24

It will all happen in a moment, in the twinkling of an eye, when the last trumpet is blown. For there will be a trumpet blast from the sky and all the Christians who have died will suddenly become alive, with new bodies that will never, never die; and then we who are still alive shall suddenly have new bodies too.
(1 CORINTHIANS 15:52 TLB)

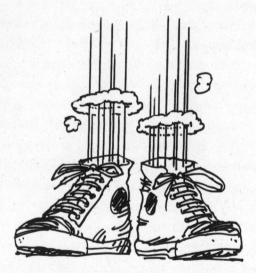

In a Moment . . .
in the twinkling of an eye. . . .

1 Corinthians 15:52

© Danny Loya

Be made new in the attitude of your minds.
(EPHESIANS 4:23)

When I was in Sacramento speaking for a women's retreat, a cheerful, perky gal in a wheelchair volunteered to help at my book table. Her name was Mary Jane, and she only had one leg. But she whirled around in that wheelchair, getting change and doing a fabulous job of handling customers who wanted to buy my books.

Later Mary Jane told me her leg had been amputated because of cancer. Then she began to laugh and said that for years her doctor had been after her to lose weight. He had put her on diets, which were always unsuccessful, and when she finally went in for the leg amputation, she said from the operating table, "Now you be sure to weigh the leg so you can remove that amount of weight from my chart!"

What an attitude! Her pain is inevitable, but she chooses to make her option something *other* than misery! She knows the value of this truth:

It's always springtime in the heart that loves God.

March 26

But thanks be to God, who always leads us in His triumph in Christ, and manifests through us the sweet aroma of the knowledge of Him in every place.
(2 CORINTHIANS 2:14 NASB)

The apostle Paul knew something about suffering. He was beaten, whipped, stoned, and shipwrecked. He lived in danger from foes and friends alike. He went without sleep, food, and water. And on top of this, he lay awake at night agonizing for the churches he had founded. Despite all this, Paul could say, "Thanks be to God!"

You may be in a tough situation, a real calamity that seems totally hopeless. But when you trust the Lord with your pain, nothing is out of control in your life. After God told the Jews He had plans for their welfare that would give them hope, He went on to say, "Then you will call upon Me and come and pray to Me, and I will listen to you. And you will seek Me and find Me, when you search for Me with all your heart" (Jeremiah 29:12–13 NASB). The Lord is faithful to protect us.

The brook would lose its song if God removed the rocks.

My eyes are ever on the LORD, for only he will release my feet from the snare. (PSALM 25:15)

Have you ever noticed that when you're over the hill, everything seems *uphill* from where you are? Stairs are steeper. Groceries are heavier. And *everything* is farther away.

And that's not all. People are less considerate. They drive so fast you're risking life and limb if you happen to pull onto the freeway in front of them. Their brakes must wear out awfully fast, the way I see them screech and swerve in my rearview mirror.

Even clothing manufacturers are becoming less civilized. Why else would they start labeling a size 6 dress as a 12? Do they think no one notices that these things no longer fit around the waist, hips, thigh, and bosom? I'd like to call up someone in authority to report this conspiracy—but the telephone company is in on it. They've printed the directories in such small type that no one could ever find a number there.

All I can do is pass along this warning: Maturity is under attack! Unless something drastic happens, pretty soon *everyone* will suffer these awful indignities.

After age forty, your "big break" will probably be a bone.

March 28

If you believe, you will receive whatever you ask for in prayer. (MATTHEW 21:22)

You can learn to be an optimist by changing the way you think about the things around you. Pessimists tend to think negatively without realizing it. It's almost as if they are on some kind of negative automatic pilot. One example I love to use is the difference in how Bill and I look at things—even the weather. On a rare, smog-free, glorious day in Southern California, I looked up at the azure blue sky and the fleecy white clouds and said, "Wow, it looks as if God vacuumed the sky."

Bill looked up at the same sky and said, "Yeah, but He'll probably dump the vacuum bag tomorrow."

To put it another way, an optimist would invent the airplane. Bill would invent the parachute! If you are one who looks for rain when there isn't a cloud in the sky, try to become alert to your automatic thoughts. Be aware of the negative things you say about yourself, others, and life—and STOP. Set your mind's automatic pilot on "optimistic" instead and make Philippians 4:8 your prayer.

A pessimist has no starter. An optimist has no brakes.

I tell you the truth, unless you change and become like little children, you will never enter the kingdom of heaven. (MATTHEW 18:3)

What mothers think of when someone suggests they can change the world.

The Lord gives us our faces, but we must provide the expression.

All hard work brings a profit, but mere talk leads only to poverty. (PROVERBS 14:23)

Dear Barbara,

My doctor insists that I must begin a vigorous exercise program. Can you suggest one?

Plump in Petoskey

Dear Plump,

The most important thing to remember about exercise is to start SLOWLY . . . and then taper off. And remember this: The easiest way to get a healthy body is to MARRY one!

There is one exercise that I tried, and it sounded so simple . . . I was supposed to bend over my vacuum cleaner and extend my right leg behind me while I touched my head to my knee. This was just before my vacuum sucked up my nightgown and caused me to completely pass out!

I had to give up jogging for my health . . . My thighs kept rubbing together and setting my pantyhose on fire!

God bought my life back from death, and I will continue to enjoy life. (JOB 33:28 NCV)

Remember that just as you have different tastes in food and clothing, you have tastes in humor. Know what kind of humor appeals to you, and look for it in films, videos, cartoons, books, and magazines. Also, seek out people who make you laugh. It may be a certain friend, or one of your children, or a grandchild. Whoever it is, spend time with that person.

Do everything you can to cultivate a sense of humor, which involves more than just telling jokes. A sense of humor is connected to the way you look at life, the way you can chuckle over what is absurd and ridiculous, the way you put your problems in perspective, and the way you can feel joy because you know that:

Any day above ground is a good one!

April 1

The wise man is glad to be instructed, but a self-sufficient fool falls flat on his face. (PROVERBS 10:8 TLB)

Happy April Fools' Day! Of all the firsts of the month I celebrate, this is the one I celebrate most foolishly. Each April I try to think of a way to surpass some of my previous goofball behaviors. For example, one time I went to the post office on the day the landscapers had trimmed the evergreens. As a kindly old gentleman opened the door for me, I sniffed the air and said merrily, "Doesn't it smell just like Christmas around here?"

Somehow we also ended up going out of the post office at the same time. I'm not sure what came over me, but I reached down and picked up a little sprig of the evergreen trimmings and put it in my mouth. With the greenery hanging out of my teeth I told him, "You know, it even TASTES like Christmas around here!"

I laughed all the way home, remembering his flabbergasted expression and savoring that smell and taste that no one else, except maybe another fractured mother, would even notice.

Some people grow up and spread cheer . . . others just grow up and spread!

We walk by faith, not by sight. (2 CORINTHIANS 5:7 NKJV)

Our son Steve and I shared the same warped sense of humor. One time he and I were driving home from church when he spotted a big, black Cadillac hearse for sale in a car lot. "Wow!" Steve exclaimed. "Wouldn't it be great to have something like that?"

I made a snap decision, wrote out a check for $350, and bought it! Steve could hardly contain himself as he drove it home. When we got there, Bill could hardly contain himself, either! It took some fast talking to get him to let Steve keep the hearse. We really couldn't afford it at the time, but the hearse was a *lot* of fun. It only got six miles to the gallon, but Steve rented it to some buddies for Halloween. They had a great time "haunting" the boulevard. I still have photos of that night, as well as pictures of Steve and his friends heading for the beach in his hearse, surfboard hanging out the back!

Those bittersweet memories are such a comfort now when we remember the real hearse that carried his body to the cemetery.

One who is filled with joy preaches without preaching.

April 3

When they walk through the Valley of Weeping it will become a place of springs where pools of blessing and refreshment collect after rains! They will grow constantly in strength. (PSALM 84:6–7 TLB)

When a lady told me her child had died and she couldn't work her retail job anymore because the tears kept coming all the time, I shared my little plan to help. I told her, "Get the saddest music tapes you can find. When everyone is out of the house, go to the bedroom, unplug the phone, turn on the sad music, flop on the bed, and SOB. Set a timer for thirty minutes and during that time cry and pound the pillow. VENTILATE. If you're angry at God, that's OK. Get those deep hurts out through the avenue of tears. Do that every day for thirty days, and every day set your timer for one minute less. After thirty days, you will have dumped a lot of your grief." Soon the lady told me she'd been taking my advice for a week and already felt again God's comfort blanket of love surrounding her.

The best way to forget your troubles . . . is to wear tight shoes.

"My food," Jesus said, *"is to do the will of him who sent me and to finish his work."* (JOHN 4:34)

The only good thing about being plump, or well-upholstered, as I like to say, is that we're not alone. Despite all the diets, weight-loss clinics, fitness clubs, and self-help books, *millions* of us are over-weight. In fact, a recent survey shows that for the first time, overweight Americans outnumber normal-sized ones.

I've been very good about watching my weight. I watch it go up and down and up and down. I heard someone call this "the rhythm method of girth control"! Actually, I *do* watch what I eat—until I get it in my mouth. Then I lose sight of it.

Erma Bombeck said she went on a seven-hundred-calorie-a-day diet in January, and "by the end of the month, I had eaten all my allotted calories through June 15." Frankly, my current diet goal is simply to heed a helpful rule someone sent me:

Never weigh more than your refrigerator.

April 5

If God holds back the waters, there is no rain; if he lets the waters go, they flood the land. He is strong and victorious; both the one who fools others and the one who is fooled belong to him. (JOB 12:15–16 NCV)

**"It's a low-cholesterol ice cream cone—
a scoop of mashed potatoes with sprinkles."**

When dieting, remember: *What's on the table eventually becomes what's on the chair.*

The angel of the LORD said, "Why do you ask my name? It is too amazing for you to understand." (JUDGES 13:18 NCV)

Even when I have to work hard at negotiating (begging and whining) to get the titles I want for my books, I enjoy every minute of it. All the whining just makes for a better story in the end, which I love to share with folks who ask, "Where in the world did you get that title?"

It's also fun to see how the titles get mangled and twisted. For example, after *He's Gonna Toot, and I'm Gonna Scoot* came out, I got an early morning call from a West Virginia lady who had heard about the book on the radio and was puzzled by the title. She thought it was *Poop 'n' Scoop.* And at my book table a woman thought the title was *Too Pooped to Scoot!* Then there was the woman who sent her husband to the bookstore to buy the book for her. She wrote, "He proceeded to go in and ask for *One More Toot and I'm Gonna Move!*"

You can judge your age by the amount of pain you feel when you come in contact with a new idea.

April 7

The more you look for humor, the more you'll find it. Try keeping a journal that notes the humorous things you've read, seen, or heard. Clip cartoons to put on your bulletin board or the family fridge. Share them with visitors and guests. You never know when you'll need something to add a little joy to your life.

Here are some funnies to get you started:

> **He who laughs last**
> **probably has an insecure upper plate.**

* * *

> **As you age, what you lose in elasticity, you gain in**
> **wisdom . . . and I think it's a real good trade-off.**

* * *

> **"Well-adjusted" means you can make the same**
> **mistakes over and over again, and keep smiling.**

April 8

Fear not, neither be discouraged. (DEUTERONOMY 1:21 KJV)

When my friend Walter Martin and two agnostics were guests on the *Phil Donahue Show*, the topics for the day included death, heaven, and the penalty for sin. As the program drew to a close, Donahue went up to Dr. Martin in his familiar way and said, "Well, now, Doc, don't you think when I get to the end of the road, God will put His arms around me and say, 'Aw, c'mon in, Phil!'?"

Dr. Martin smiled and responded, "Oh, Phil, He already did—two thousand years ago! He invited you to come on in THEN!" This story brings tears to my eyes as I realize how God made it possible for us to be assured of heaven because of His loving sacrifice for us. We have an open invitation with a heavenly RSVP.

Walter is now with the Lord, but his response to Phil Donahue that day is a splash of joy that continues to encourage me whenever I think of it, giving me extra courage when I need it. Truly, our WORDS OF FAITH go on long after we're gone.

There's no better gift we can give others than the hope of heaven!

April 9

The days of our life are seventy years, . . . even then their span is only toil and trouble; they are soon gone and we fly away. (PSALM 90:10 NRSV)

Holding a rock-solid belief about the glory to come for us and our loved ones not only empowers Christians here on earth to endure tough times, it also inspires us to accomplish great things. For example, songwriter Albert Brumley dreamed of flying away to heaven as he toiled at picking cotton in 1928. The result was Brumley's simple but classic hymn "I'll Fly Away." It's a simple song with a powerful message, and it has been recognized as the most recorded gospel song in history.

At the end of our lives here on earth, as Christians, our souls "fly away" to heaven. When we think of "R.I.P." carved on a Christian's tombstone, we don't think "rest in peace" but "rejoicing in paradise"!

Epitaph over a dentist's grave: *He is filling his last cavity.*

*God, save me, because the water has risen to my neck.
I'm sinking down into the mud, and there is nothing to
stand on. . . . I am tired from calling for help; my throat
is sore. . . . God, because of your great love, answer me.
You are truly able to save.* (PSALM 69:1–3, 13 NCV)

THE FAMILY CIRCUS.   **By Bil Keane**

"I know why the car pool's so late, Mommy! This
is OUR morning to drive!"

April 11

And now these three remain: faith, hope and love. But the greatest of these is love. (1 CORINTHIANS 13:13)

Folks often ask me, "Barb, where do you get your joy?" That question always makes me think of 1 Corinthians 13, the "love chapter." With so many cesspools to fall into in life, we need a spring we can go to for splashes of joy—a spring full of living water that only Jesus provides.

As Tony Campolo says: "It's Friday, but Sunday's Comin'." On that first Good Friday, Jesus' followers were in a real cesspool. Jesus had been crucified, and now He was dead. Then the temple veil split open, rocks moved, tombs opened up, and the Roman centurion who had overseen the execution babbled, "This WAS the Son of God!"

Then came Sunday. Mary Magdalene and the other women found the stone rolled away from the tomb and an angel in blazing white saying, "He is not here—He is risen!" On Friday all had been darkness, despair, and grief. But on Sunday the whole world had cause for joy greater than any known before or since.

We aren't just Easter people living in a Good Friday world. We are RESURRECTION people!

And I know that after this body has decayed, this body shall see God! Then he will be on my side! Yes, I shall see him, not as a stranger, but as a friend! What a glorious hope! (JOB 19:26–27 TLB)

The counselor who helped me when my life was so bleak once wrote to me to say that my ministry encourages people to survive their losses. And then he added:

Even dying people die more graciously when they have hope, either for recovery or for heaven.

That's a good thought! In fact, it's burned into my memory, and I see its wisdom confirmed in my mail, which constantly reminds me of the power of hope. When heartbroken parents reach out to me for help, I admit to them there were plenty of times when I, too, was ready to fold up and move into the Home for the Bewildered. But somehow God kept me going, always helping me find something positive, even something humorous, to get me through each day.

Death is God's way of saying, "Your table is ready."

April 13

The ways of God are without fault; the LORD's words are pure. He is a shield to those who trust him.
(2 SAMUEL 22:31 NCV)

Lord, I ask more questions
Than You ask.
The ratio, I would suppose,
Is ten to one.

I ask:
Why do You permit this anguish?
How long can I endure it?
What possible purpose does it serve?
Have You forgotten to be gracious?
Have I wearied You?
Have I offended You?
Have You cast me off?
Where did I miss Your guidance?
When did I lose the way?
Do You see my utter despair?

You ask:
Are you trusting Me?

—RUTH HARMS CALKIN

For the good man—the blameless, the upright, the man of peace—he has a wonderful future ahead of him. For him there is a happy ending. (PSALM 37:37 TLB)

Dr. Charles Swindoll is one of the most optimistic, "up" people I have ever met. He always has a smile and loves to laugh. He is a living, breathing example of the power of attitude. In his book *Strengthening Your Grip,* he wrote:

> We have a choice every day regarding the attitude we will embrace for that day. We cannot change our past . . . we cannot change the fact that people will act in a certain way. We cannot change the inevitable. The only thing we can do is play on the one string we have, and that is our attitude.

Play on your one string as optimistically as you can. Make the best of it, even when you get the worst of it—and never forget that every day holds the possibility of miracles.

Optimism is having three teenage sons . . .
and only one car.

Jesus . . . said, "It is not the healthy people who need a doctor, but the sick." (MATTHEW 9:11 NCV)

A story for tax day from Luke 19:1–10 (TM):

Then Jesus entered and walked through Jericho. There was a man there, his name Zacchaeus, the head tax man and quite rich. He wanted desperately to see Jesus, but the crowd was in his way—he was a short man and couldn't see over the crowd. So he ran on ahead and climbed up in a sycamore tree so he could see Jesus when he came by.

When Jesus got to the tree, he looked up and said, "Zacchaeus, hurry down. Today is my day to be a guest in your home." . . . Everyone who saw the incident was indignant and grumped, "What business does he have getting cozy with this crook?"

Zacchaeus . . . stammered apologetically, "Master, I give away half my income to the poor—and if I'm caught cheating, I pay four times the damages."

Jesus said, "Today is salvation day in this home! Here he is: Zacchaeus, son of Abraham! For the Son of Man came to find and restore the lost."

When you do a good deed, get a receipt—in case heaven is like the IRS.

Remember your Creator now while you are young.
(ECCLESIASTES 12:6 TLB)

A little boy told his preschool teacher one morning, "I have a disappointment to talk about in circle time."

"Ohhhh," said his teacher, worried he might spill some devastating family news. "Could you tell me first?"

"No," he replied solemnly. "I want to tell everyone."

She tried to persuade him to give her a preview of his disappointment, but he stubbornly refused to say another word until his little classmates were assembled in the sharing-time circle. Nervously, the teacher waited. When it was his turn, the little boy took a breath and told about lying down on a big chair that lifted him up toward a bright light. A man wearing a mask told him to open his mouth and then tapped on his teeth with something hard, he said. It was then the preschool teacher realized just what the little tyke was describing: his *dentist appointment.*

A woman took her small daughter to the funeral home for the viewing of her great-grandmother. Staring, perplexed, into the casket, the little girl asked, "Mama, why did they put Great-grandma in a jewelry box?"

April 17

The kingdom of heaven is like a mustard seed. . . . Though it is the smallest of all your seeds, yet when it grows, it is the largest of garden plants and becomes a tree.
(MATTHEW 13:31–32)

We *all* need some little something to brighten our lives now and then. When a devastating earthquake struck Southern California, one woman wrote to tell me how some little "splashes of joy" marbles I'd handed out at a retreat reminded her to keep on smiling through her tears. She said she put them on the window sill and forgot about them.

But their message of Jesus' love came to me as I was cleaning a huge mess of broken things after the earthquake.

Everything had broken into millions of pieces. I was sad, scared, and upset as I cleaned. Then I saw a "sparkle" among my broken treasures. I cried as I scooped up the little sparkle stone and thanked God that I had been able to have those treasures for the years I had enjoyed them. I thought, "For this I have Jesus." Thank you, Barbara, for this reminder that Jesus loves me. I'll sparkle for Him.

Life is wonderful . . . do your best not to miss it!

Oh, that they would always have such a heart for me, wanting to obey my commandments. Then all would go well with them in the future, and with their children throughout all generations! (DEUTERONOMY 5:29 TLB)

M y heart has been wrung out so many times it's bound to be wrinkled! But I am continually rejuvenated by the laughter I find all around me—even from the parents who write to me after they've landed on the ceiling and need someone to lovingly scrape them off with a spatula of love.

For example, one woman wrote to me the day after she'd learned that her son was gay. In her state of shock, she wasn't even sure she could write the word *homosexual*. She said, "Barbara, I can't even spell—is that a clear sign of my condition?"

Freshly shocked parents usually believe they will never recover from the trauma, and they certainly don't ever expect to laugh again. But gradually they, too, learn to see humor all around them.

Warning! *Humor may be hazardous to your depression.*

April 19

Oh, that I had the wings of a dove! I would fly away and be at rest. (PSALM 55:6)

A touching story reminded me of the promise of heaven when Swissair Flight 111 crashed off the coast of Nova Scotia a couple of years ago. One of the 229 passengers killed in the crash was Jonathan Wilson, a twenty-two-year-old man who was heading for Geneva to work with the Youth With A Mission ministry. The parting words Jonathan spoke to this family when he left Florida would later take on a double meaning that reminded them he had flown away—not to Europe but to heaven. He told his family he would "be there until the Lord called him home."

This remarkable story proves the point of a little clipping someone sent me recently. To nonbelievers, it's just a joke. To Christians, it's glorious truth:

When traveling by plane, the Christian said, "If we go down, I go up!"

Commit everything you do to the Lord. Trust him to help you do it and he will. (PSALM 37:5 TLB)

When I said those words, "Whatever, Lord," it seemed to release a million little sparkles inside me. The shag rug came out of my throat, my teeth stopped itching, and the elephant got up off my chest for the first time in eleven months. All I'd said was, "Whatever, Lord," instead of my usual, "Why me? Why *my* son? Why is *my* life such a mess?" Suddenly all the heaviness was GONE!

For me, saying "Whatever, Lord," was like Job saying, "Though he slay me, yet will I trust in him" (Job 13:15 KJV). I turned my car around, left the viaduct, and for the first time in eleven months I could take a deep breath. I sang all the way home—"The King Is Coming" and "Come on Down, Lord Jesus." I hadn't sung for eleven months, but that day I sang my heart out.

Thoughts of you are "hallelujahs!" in the choir loft of my mind.

April 21

*We do not know how to pray as we should. But the
Spirit himself speaks to God for us, even begs God for
us with deep feelings that words cannot explain.*
(ROMANS 8:26 NCV)

Our son Larry disappeared after we discovered he
was a homosexual and argued with him during
a bitter confrontation. For several months I stayed in
my bedroom and counted the roses on the wallpaper. I
felt like a zombie, a zero with the rim rubbed out. I even
considered driving off a high viaduct near Disneyland
and killing myself. But once I was up there, I worried,
*What if I'm just maimed and crippled and making baskets for
the rest of my life?*

I sat in the car and prayed, "Lord, I'm taking an
imaginary hammer, and I'm going to nail Larry to the
cross, because I can't handle this anymore. I'm tired of
this elephant on my chest, my teeth itching, and this
rug in my throat. I'm giving him to You. And if I never
see him again, *whatever, Lord—whatever happens*—I'm
nailing him to the cross and giving him to YOU!"

"Whatever, Lord!" That *is* the prayer of relinquishment!

Teach me your way, O LORD; lead me in a straight path because of my oppressors. (PSALM 27:11)

When calamity comes, the wicked are brought down,
but even in death the righteous have a refuge.
(PROVERBS 14:32)

My good friend Marilyn Meberg always has a happy thought to share. One of her favorites is, "We're all marching relentlessly to the grave." Isn't that delightful?

To stave off that inevitable fact, we try to use face-lifts, tummy tucks, hair coloring—anything to avoid the fact that age is taking its toll on us. We spend millions trying to deny what is happening to our bodies as we acquire various physical limitations. When our eyesight fails, we wear glasses. When our hearing goes, we adapt to hearing aids. And when our minds go . . . then we're REALLY in trouble!

Death stalks all of us, but as Christians, we have an advantage over nonbelievers: We can look death in the face . . . and laugh.

I have a great diet. You're allowed to eat anything you want, but you must eat it in the company of naked fat people.

He is wooing you from the jaws of distress to a spacious place free from restriction, to the comfort of your table laden with choice food. (JOB 36:16)

The Twenty-Third Cupcake

My doctor is my shepherd; I shall not weigh more.

He maketh me to lie down in green sweatpants; he ordereth me to do situps. He specify-eth my goal. He sendeth me down jogging trails of endless length for my heart's sake.

Yea, though I stroll by the door of the bakeshop, I will not enter; my sweetrolls and crumbcake I secretly buy elsewhere.

I eatest my cupcakes in the presence of no one. I feast on rich Twinkies and Ding-Dongs. My cup's full of ice cream.

Surely huge hips and thunder thighs will haunt me all the days of my life, and I will live in a body of cellulite forever.

—ANN LUNA

One of the problems with diets is the first three letters spell "die"!

April 25

Children are a gift from God; they are his reward.
(PSALM 127:3 TLB)

Some time ago, a tiny three-year-old daughter used a whole roll of gold wrapping paper to wrap a present for her father. Money was tight for the family, and when the little girl brought the gift to him, her father winced to see how much of the expensive paper had been used. Then his anger flared when he found that the box, so elaborately wrapped, was completely empty.

"Don't you know that when you give someone a present, there's supposed to be something inside of it?" he snapped. "You've wasted all this paper on an empty box."

The little girl looked up at him with tears in her eyes and said, "Oh, Daddy! It's not empty. I blew kisses into the box. They're for you, Daddy."

Each of us parents has been given a gold box filled with unconditional love from our children. There is no more precious possession anyone could hold.

The only condition for loving is to love without conditions.

The Lord is my light and my salvation; whom shall I fear? (PSALM 27:1 TLB)

After a rather impressive Southern California earthquake, my sister, Janet, came out from Minnesota to visit us. Because of the recent shaker, she was rather apprehensive. One morning Janet put a few things in the washer, not knowing if the load was too light the washer was easily thrown off balance.

We were sitting at the kitchen table, chatting, when we suddenly heard all kinds of BOOMING and BUMP-ING noises. Then our mobile home began to SHAKE. My first thought was EARTHQUAKE! "Get under the table QUICK!" I shouted to Janet.

We were both struggling to get ourselves under the table when I began suspecting what was really wrong. I staggered over to open the utility room door just as the washer propelled itself into the next cycle. The booming and shaking stopped. I said, "It's just the washer."

Soon we were both laughing hysterically. It was a good example of how close to the ragged edge we live here in Southern California. Any time we feel any kind of shaking we think, "IT'S THE BIG ONE!"

Good sense is easier to have than to use.

Give great joy to all who wish me well. Let them shout with delight, "Great is the Lord who enjoys helping his child!" (PSALM 35:27 TLB)

I'm not sure why it's curative to hear that other people are enduring more severe problems than we are, and I certainly don't claim to have any healing properties myself. But I've been through a lot of heartache over the last twenty years. And I'm not out of the cesspool yet. In fact, when one woman heard about my ongoing struggles, she wrote:

You and Job...
have so much in common...
henceforth
You will be called
JOBELLA !

Prayer is asking for rain. Faith is carrying an umbrella.

This, at least, gives me comfort despite all the pain—
that I have not denied the words of the holy God.
(JOB 6:10 TLB)

I love the nickname "Jobella," because it reminds me of all that poor old Job went through—and still he was steadfast in his faith, knowing he would survive. He said, "Though He slay me, yet will I trust Him" (Job 13:15 NJKV). Job knew his troubles would end someday. Then, he knew, God would "fill [his] mouth with laughter and [his] lips with shouts of joy" (Job 8:21).

Like Job, I know my problems won't last forever. But sometimes that day seems a long way off. Just when Bill and I think things are as bad as they could possibly be—when we've finally made it to safe harbor—another hurricane comes along. One letter writer put it well when she said:

Help! We need a giant spatula! My husband says he feels like one of those moving ducks in a penny arcade. We just pop up, thinking blissfully that the worst is over . . . and *bang!* We get shot down again.

A day without sunshine is like, well, night.

April 29

The angel carried me away by the Spirit to a very large and high mountain. He showed me the holy city, Jerusalem, coming down out of heaven from God.
(REVELATION 21:10 NCV)

While we're not really sure where heaven is, the Bible often refers to it as being *up* or *above*. That produces one of the "side effects" of heavenly thinking. When we're focusing on the joy we'll know in heaven, our thoughts turn heavenward—that's upward. Our hopes rise, and life down here is more bearable.

Picturing the happy reunion we'll have someday in that "land beyond the river that we call the sweet forever" brings tears of joy to my eyes. And some of us may have an even greater capacity for rejoicing up there. As Randy Alcorn said, "All of us will be full of joy in heaven, but some may have more joy because their capacity [has] been stretched through their trust in and obedience to God in this life." How comforting to know the hole left by the loss of loved ones will be filled in heaven with "joy, joy, joy, joy down in my heart"!

May the joybells of heaven ding-dong in your heart today!

But his delight is in the law of the LORD, / And in His law he meditates day and night. (PSALM 1:2 NASB)

Most of us miss out on life's big prizes:

> The Pulitzer
> The Heisman
> Oscars
> The Nobel prize

But we all qualify for life's small pleasures:

> A pat on the back
> A kiss on the cheek
> A five-pound bass
> A full moon
> An empty parking space
> A crackling fire
> A great meal
> A glorious sunset

Enjoy life's tiny delights. There are plenty for all of us.

Love cures people—both the ones who give it and the ones who receive it.

May 1

A woman has ten valuable silver coins and loses one.
Won't she . . . look in every corner of the house . . . until
she finds it? (LUKE 15:8 TLB)

Before Bill and I rode our bikes to the doughnut shop one morning, I tucked a twenty-dollar bill in my pocket. We ordered maple bars and coffee, and when the girl brought it, I gave her my twenty, then she disappeared to the back to get cream. When she returned, she asked for $2.50. She didn't speak much English, and when I said we had already paid, she kept saying we hadn't. Since we hadn't brought along any more money and we'd already munched on the pastries, we sighed and sat down to finish them. Bill was upset that our treat had cost twenty dollars. But as we rode home, I remembered a twenty-dollar bill we had *found* a year earlier. With his melancholy temperament, Bill chose to harbor ill feelings. But the way I looked at it, this was the same twenty dollars I had found—and we really got the maple bars for free!

Don't forget to celebrate the first of the month!

Even in laughter the heart may be in pain.
(PROVERBS 14:13 NASB)

Humor helps to combat my own grief and helps me accelerate the grief process for others. I love little quips and quotes and have collected hundreds of them over the years. Folks need something that will help get them through the times when nothing seems to calm them, not even reminders of comfort from the Bible given by well-meaning Christian friends. It's not that these verses aren't true; it's just that the pain is so intense you can't appreciate what the words are saying at that moment. Later these scriptures can become meaningful again, but, ironically, there were times during my own grief that the following observation made a kind of crazy sense to me:

> Man cannot live by bread alone;
> he needs peanut butter, too.

I guess I try to be the eternal optimist. And you know the difference between an optimist and a pessimist, don't you?

An optimist is someone who thinks he knows a friend from whom he can borrow. A pessimist is one who has tried.

May 3

Suddenly there was a great earthquake; for an angel of the Lord came down from heaven and rolled aside the stone and sat on it. (MATTHEW 28:2 TLB)

I still laugh when I remember the time an earthquake hit our area of Southern California while two local TV newscasters were broadcasting. As the studio shook and the big lights overhead start swaying, their eyes grew wide, and then the two men disappeared from sight. *From under their newsdesk,* they continued giving the story of the latest earthquake to hit the area!

Now, having lived through several earthquakes myself, I understand just how they felt. When an earthquake strikes, you'll dive under anything to protect yourself. After my sister, Janet, and I dived under the kitchen table when my unbalanced washing machine made our mobile home shake, I realized just how skittish we all are about these quakes! But how we laughed afterward. Now I'm tempted to try it again anytime we have out-of-state company over just to see them run for cover!

An expert knows all the answers . . . if you ask the right questions.

The LORD is God. He is God in heaven above and on the earth below. There is no other god! (DEUTERONOMY 4:39 NCV)

We hope the Lord will return for us soon, but there's no way we can know *when* the Rapture will occur. So we have to be ready to fly away to heaven at any moment, because, as someone said, the trumpet hasn't sounded yet, but the trumpeter is surely warming up!

For that reason (and a few others!) I won't be making reservations with the Seattle company that a few years ago started selling tickets for a rocket-ship ride in the year 2001. The clipping describing this caper (sent by a friend who knows my longing to "fly away") says that, on the first day reservations were accepted, fifteen people plopped down a $5,000 deposit for the three-hour trip, which will ultimately cost each passenger nearly $100,000!

While those daredevils will fly sixty-two miles above the earth, my journey will take me much farther than that; I'm heading all the way to eternity! And there's another important difference: We'll both be headed *up*. But I won't be coming back *down!*

Life is uncertain. Eat dessert first!

The secret of the LORD *is for those who fear Him.*
(PSALM 25:14 NASB)

Like Job, I know my problems won't last forever. To remind myself of this, I frequently quote that wonderful King James phrase that reminds me my trouble didn't come to STAY. Again and again in that beautiful old version, the words appear: "It came to PASS."

Of course, there ARE exceptions to this "came-to-pass" rule, especially the mysterious staying power of a phenomenon that occurs in chocolate shops:

How is it that you can gain two pounds by eating half a pound of fudge?

While you're pondering this imponderable, here are a few more:

- *Why are there* **interstate** *highways in Hawaii?*
- *If you tied jellied toast to the back of a cat and dropped the cat, would the toast land jelly-side down or would the cat land on its feet?*
- *Why do we drive on* **parkways** *and park in* **driveways?**

And it came to pass at the end of forty days, that Noah opened the window of the ark which he had made.
(GENESIS 8:6 KJV)

This Too Shall Pass

Looking on the bright side of life will never cause eyestrain.

May 7

The bread of God is he who comes down from heaven and gives life to the world. (JOHN 6:33)

A doctor who had devoted his life to helping the poor lived over a grocery store in the ghetto of a large city. In front of the grocery store was a sign reading "Dr. Williams Is Upstairs."

When he died, he had no relatives, and he left no money for his burial. He had never asked for payment from anyone he had ever treated.

The doctor's friends and patients scraped enough money together to bury the good doctor, but they had no money for a tombstone. It appeared that his grave was going to be unmarked until someone came up with a wonderful suggestion. They took the sign from in front of the grocery store and nailed it to a post over his grave. It made a lovely epitaph: *Dr. Williams Is Upstairs.*

Overheard at a doctor's office: *"Dear me, I've been waiting so long I think I've recovered!"*

The real mother of the living child was full of love for her son. So she said to the king, "Please, my master, don't kill him! Give the baby to her!" (1 KINGS 3:26 NCV)

May is the month of Mother's Day, so for the coming week let's focus on mothers—either our own mother, or our current role.

You know you're a mother when . . .

- You have time to shave only one leg at a time.
- You've mastered the art of placing large quantities of different foods on a plate without anything touching.
- You hear your mother's voice coming out of your mouth.
- You use your own saliva to clean your child's face.

The rooster may crow, but it's the hen who delivers the goods.

May 9

Then the angel said to her, "Do not be afraid, Mary, for you have found favor with God. And behold, you will conceive in your womb and bring forth a Son, and shall call His name Jesus." (LUKE 1:30–31 NKJV)

Becoming a parent changes everything, but parenthood itself also changes with each baby. For example, consider your wardrobe. As soon as the pregnancy test kit confirms that you're pregnant, you head for the mall—and come home wearing a maternity outfit. With the second baby, you squeeze into your regular clothes as long as possible.

With the third baby, your maternity clothes *are* your regular clothes!

Then there's your preparation for labor and delivery. With the first baby you attend weekly classes and faithfully practice your breathing. With the second baby, you try to keep breathing when you find your two-year-old teetering at the top of the basement stairs.

With the third baby, you threaten to hold your breath indefinitely unless the doctor gives you an epidural in your second trimester!

Two things every mom needs: *Velcro arms and a Teflon heart.*

Great peace have they who love your law, and nothing can make them stumble. (PSALM 119:165)

Mother's Day perfume is kind of an all-purpose gift. It pleases mothers one day a year—and kills mosquitoes the rest. —NELSON'S BIG BOOK OF LAUGHTER

May 11

Lord, how you have helped me before! You took me safely from my mother's womb and brought me through the years of infancy. I have depended upon you since birth; you have always been my God. (PSALM 22:9–10 TLB)

A new baby can cause overwhelming fatigue, so parents adapt different stress-coping strategies with each child. For instance, with the first baby, you worry so much about the baby's cries that you never put the infant down—you wear him constantly in a baby carrier strapped to your chest. When the second baby cries, you pick him up only when his hysterics threaten to wake up your firstborn. With the third child, you teach your other two kids where to look for the pacifier and how to rewind the baby swing.

Parents' dealings with baby-sitters also change. The first time you leave your baby with a sitter, you train the caregiver for two hours then call home four times while you run to the post office. With the second baby, you remember to leave an emergency phone number—your neighbor's. With the third baby, you tell the sitter to call only if someone needs stitches, splints, or an ambulance.

A mother is God's deputy on earth.

I am calm and quiet, like a baby with its mother. I am at peace, like a baby with its mother. (PSALM 131:2 NCV)

Baby activities change with each additional child. You take your first infant to baby swim classes, baby aerobics, and baby massage. You take your second baby to baby story hour so you can nap while the story is read. You take the third baby to the McDonald's drive-through.

You use your time differently as each child comes along. You spend hours each day staring adoringly at your precious firstborn. With the second baby, you glance in her direction occasionally as you race to stop your toddler from dropping the cat down the laundry chute. With the third child, you train the dog to guard the baby from his siblings a few hours each day while you hide in the closet.

A baby is a small member of the family who can make the love stronger, the days shorter, the nights longer, and the bankroll smaller. When a baby is born the home will be happier—even if the clothes are shabbier. The past is forgotten, and the future is worth living for.

May 13

Hope deferred makes the heart sick; but when dreams come true at last, there is life and joy. (PROVERBS 13:12 TLB)

It was an extra-busy Monday, early in May 1986. I had just returned from speaking at a three-day women's conference and now I was back home, hurriedly getting ready to leave again almost immediately for an extended trip to Minnesota.

The trip meant being gone for Mother's Day, but that didn't matter. Barney and his family were going to drop by later to share their gifts and hugs. And Larry . . . well, Larry had been gone without a word or trace for years, so I was getting used to it.

In the midst of my packing, the phone rang. It was Larry! The voice I had longed to hear for so many years said, "I want to come over and give you a Mother's Day present." He came and stayed for more than two hours, and we laughed and cried and hugged and shared. Hope had been deferred for me for eleven years. But my dream came true at last, and there was overwhelming joy when my prodigal son came home.

Joy is God living in the marrow of your bones.

You helped me even on the day of my birth. I will always praise you. I am an example to many people, because you are my strong protection. (PSALM 71:6–7 NCV)

We mothers of multiple children like to say we love all our kids equally, but in our heart of hearts, we know that's not true. It's how the mother of several children answered when a reporter asked her, "Which of your children do you love the most?"

The wise and loving mother replied, "I love the one most who is away from home until he returns, the one who is sick until he is well, the one who is hurt until the hurt disappears, and the one who is lost until he is found." —ADAPTED FROM ALICE GRAY, *STORIES FOR A WOMAN'S HEART.*

Who are these kids . . . and why are they calling me MOM?

May 15

My child, listen to your father's teaching and do not forget your mother's advice. (PROVERBS 1:8 NCV)

If you're wondering whether you have what it takes to be a mother, here are three tests to help you get ready:

Preparation for Pregnancy: From the food co-op, obtain a twenty-five-pound bag of pinto beans and attach it to your waist with a belt. Wear it everywhere you go for nine months. Then remove ten of the beans to indicate the baby has been born.

Mess-Management Preparation: Smear grape jelly on the living room furniture and curtains. Now plunge your hands into a bag of potting soil, wipe them on the walls, and highlight the smudges with Magic Markers.

Inhalation Therapy Preparation: Empty a carton of milk onto the cloth upholstery of the family van, park the vehicle in a sunny spot, and leave it to ripen for the month of August. Rub a half-finished frozen fudge bar through your hair, then hide it in the glove compartment.

The mother's heart is the child's schoolroom.

—HENRY WARD BEECHER

Have faith in the LORD your God and you will be upheld.
(2 CHRONICLES 20:20)

T wo things got me through all the agonies I've faced: a tattered but enduring faith in God and a wacky sense of humor. I also learned a lot from parents whose letters pour into my mailbox. While some letters are anguished cries from parents who've just landed on the ceiling, many others are from those who've finally emerged from life's cesspool. Now they're eager to throw a lifeline to others still swirling through the sludge. They know:

> TO LOVE AND BE LOVED IS TO FEEL
> THE SUN ON BOTH SIDES OF OURSELVES.

As one mother wrote:

Since our world was turned upside down by the news that our daughter is a lesbian, God has done so much healing. . . . As I've read so many times from other parents, He has changed my heart and given me a capacity for love that is miraculous!

Sign painted on house destroyed by earthquake:
"The fat lady has sung."

> *Then the king was deeply moved, and . . . wept. . . .*
> *He said thus: "O my son Absalom—my son, my son*
> *Absalom—if only I had died in your place!"*
> (2 SAMUEL 18:33 NKJV)

The mother of a gay son said her holidays used to be ruined because she wanted what she could not have: "a family like other people have." Fortunately she found a way to ease her pain:

My birthday, Easter, and Mother's Day have come and gone. . . . Like David . . . I continued to grieve for the lost life of my son while I made my friends feel that no one was as important to me as he was.

Then God . . . made me see . . . that the sin of one person was ruining my life. That made all the difference this Mother's Day. I sent cards to all the new mothers I knew and to my young friends who care about me when it hurts. I even accepted a dinner invitation and took lilacs and candy to my hostess, a lady in her eighties, and had a great day.

To pull yourself out of the pit, reach out to someone else.

Treasure wisdom, and it will make you great; hold on to it, and it will bring you honor. It will be like flowers in your hair and like a beautiful crown on your head.
(PROVERBS 4:8–9 NCV)

One of my favorite Scripture verses talks about blessings for those who persevere under trials. It says when they have stood the test, they will receive "the crown of life that God has promised to those who love him" (James 1:12). There is also a song about having "stars in my crown," which would be a special joy . . . I guess.

Still, I had to laugh when a friend wrote me to say, "I love you, Barbara, for all you've done while on the earth. Maybe someday I'll be able to give you a big hug. But if I don't see you on this earth, I'll see you in heaven. I know I'll recognize you. You'll be the one with the hunched-over back from the weight of your crown."

Patience is better than strength. (PROVERBS 16:32 NCV)

After hearing me complain recently that someone's behavior had nearly sent me to the Home for the Bewildered, a friend sagely remarked: "Barbara, some people are only alive because it's illegal to kill them!"

It's true. We have all sorts of problems—and problem people—to contend with while we're waiting for God to take us home. And for people with an impatient temperament, the waiting itself is hard enough to contend with!

We all seem to struggle with impatience. A newspaper article recently reported that the lack of patience has become such a problem that "it wouldn't be surprising if a twelve-step program were introduced any day now. Call it IA—Impatients Anonymous." Some folks I know won't even buy frozen dinners if they take longer than five minutes in the microwave!

Even when a pail of water seems full, it can take many drops more. So it is with kindness. Most people appreciate even one deed of kindness, but some find it difficult to show their appreciation. Don't let this stop you. Eventually you'll do some little thing that will make their hearts overflow.

The Lord of Hosts will spread a wondrous feast for everyone around the world—a delicious feast of good food. . . . At that time he will remove the cloud of gloom, the pall of death that hangs over the earth; he will swallow up death forever. (ISAIAH 25:6–8 TLB)

For some of us, everything we do reminds us of food, even reading Scripture! We see a baby's cute little toes, and we think of bite-size Tootsie Rolls. We notice the wrinkles in an old man's smile and think of prunes. We pull our pantyhose over our thighs and think of cottage cheese. We gaze at snow-capped mountain peaks and see chocolate-marshmallow sundaes. It never ends! We can't even look at a traffic light in December without wondering whether the red and green M&Ms are in the stores yet.

It's a constant challenge to keep my mind off food—but I'm not quite as bad as those folks who equate eating with a divine encounter. In a newspaper interview one person said, "Food is the closest thing to God because it brings everyone together and puts a smile on everyone's face."

Diet tip: *If you fatten up everyone else around you, you'll look thinner.*

May 21

When you give a feast, invite the poor, the crippled, the lame, and the blind. Then you will be blessed, because they have nothing and cannot pay you back. But you will be repaid when the good people rise from the dead.
(LUKE 14:13–14 NCV)

YOU'VE HEARD OF THE ESTROGEN PATCH?

NOW THERE'S SOMETHING NEW... THE DIET PATCH!

To every thing there is a season, and a time to every purpose under the heaven. (ECCLESIASTES 3:1 KJV)

Smiling between disasters is a good start in finding splashes of joy, but surviving in the cesspool—and eventually climbing out—takes the ability to deal with pain and grief. Nothing comes into our lives by accident; and no matter how bad it makes you feel, remember: It didn't come to stay—it came to pass!

The hard part is dealing with being alive while waiting for whatever it is to pass. When pain and grief capsize your life, it sometimes seems that all you can do is sink. The letters I get from heartbroken parents help me understand why I went through my own cesspools of pain. Those terrible times helped me earn the credentials that now enable me to help others deal with their pain. And the help I offer them becomes a boomerang blessing of hope for me, too.

Things not to do when you're feeling blue: *Don't weigh yourself. Don't get your hair cut. Don't open a box of chocolates. Don't go swimsuit shopping!*

Children, come and listen to me. I will teach you to worship the LORD. (PSALM 34:11 NCV)

Actress Meryl Streep commented recently, "You don't really read the results of [your mothering efforts] until way late in life. Usually, it's the adult child who looks back and thinks: *How did she do all of that? How did she stay in a good mood all the time?* . . . If you're a mom, you know how much you're doing, but you're not going to get a lot of credit for it. Mothering is an invisible achievement."

Mothers need all the help they can get these days to reach this "invisible achievement," even though a recent study showed that "motherhood may actually make women smarter" due to prenatal hormones that "dramatically enrich parts of the brain involved in learning and memory." When I saw that, I thought, *Wow! Just when we're so exhausted we can hardly remember our own names, we're actually Einsteins in training!* Now if we could just update the theory of relativity while changing diapers, scraping *Star Wars* stickers off the car windows, and counting sprinkles on cupcakes so no one is shortchanged—we'd have it made!

Raising teenagers is like nailing Jell-O to the wall.

Only one thing concerns me: Be sure that you live in a
way that brings honor to the Good News of Christ.
(PHILIPPIANS 1:27 NCV)

Most parents who write to me are mothers, but one of the most hope-filled letters came from the father of a homosexual son. It had been two years since they'd learned their son was gay, he said, and he felt compelled to share their progress, hoping it would "offer some encouragement to others who travel our road."

He spoke of "insights we gained by immersing ourselves in the love of those who shared and understood our hurt. This gave us an opportunity to pour our hearts out in a nonthreatening, nonjudgmental atmosphere, without fear of criticism. Also, we received the assurance from others that we *would* survive!"

They reached a milestone, he said, when they "stopped focusing on straightening out our child and acknowledged that that was God's role: He fixes 'em. We love 'em."

The mind is like a television: When it goes blank, it's a good idea to turn off the sound.

Be joyful always; pray continually, give thanks in all circumstances, for this is God's will for you in Christ Jesus. (1 THESSALONIANS 5:16–18)

The apostle Paul believed that feeling joyful or miserable depends on how you look at your circumstances. We can look on the bright side or search for clouds.

Your attitude can set the mood for your home or office or even the bus or train you ride to and from work. Remember the story of the frustrated man who boarded a crowded bus after work and kept hearing an unseen passenger comment on the beautiful spring scenery, the magnificent church, the lovely park, and other landmarks? As the man exited the bus, he saw the man who was speaking—and he was blind!

"I stepped off that bus, and suddenly all my built-up tensions drained away," the man said. "God in His wisdom had sent a blind man to help see that when all seems dark and dreary it is still a beautiful world."

Be open-minded, but not so open-minded that your brains fall out!

My sheep listen to my voice; I know them, and they follow me. I give them eternal life, and they shall never perish; no one can snatch them out of my hand.
(JOHN 10:27–28)

Perhaps the hardest situation occurs when a loved one takes his or her own life. When talking to the grieving survivors, I prefer to believe that even suicide doesn't negate a person's salvation. I agree with Bible teacher Dr. Paul R. Van Gorder, who said, "Salvation depends entirely upon the grace of God. . . . Once we have received it as a gift, we are not in danger of losing it for some unconfessed sin. . . .We do not know what happens in a human mind that causes a person to take his own life. But we do know this: If that person was genuinely saved, he will 'never perish.' Though he may succeed in his suicide attempt, he will continue to have the gift of eternal life."

In difficult times, we hold tight to the promise that God loves our children even more than we do.

May 27

The One enthroned in heaven laughs. (PSALM 2:4)

Laughter CAN be contagious, not to mention unpredictable. As somebody said, perhaps laughter is the cheapest luxury we have. It stirs up the blood, expands the chest, electrifies the nerves, clears away the cobwebs from the brain, and gives the whole system a cleansing rehabilitation. A good laugh is the best medicine, whether you are sick or not. In fact:

LAUGHTER IS TO LIFE
WHAT SALT IS TO AN EGG.

That's why I sprinkle my books with all kinds of humor, from bloopers and malapropisms to crazy stories I've collected through the years. My goal is to invoke a chuckle—or maybe even a belly laugh. By the way, did you know that another name for a belly laugh is a *MIRTHQUAKE?*

Updated Witticisms:

- *Lightning never strikes twice . . . but isn't once enough?*

- *A bird in the hand . . . will poop in the palm.*

- *Silence is not just golden. It's darned hard to come by when you have kids.* —SHERRIE WEAVER

Wait for the LORD; be strong and take heart and wait for the LORD. (PSALM 27:14)

Here in Southern California, one of the places where we have to do a lot of waiting is in traffic jams. The only good thing about going nowhere on one of our multilane freeways is that it gives me a good excuse to let my mind wander. (Of course, it sometimes wanders off completely, leaving me sitting there wondering where it's wandered to—and wondering where I was going when I started!)

Whenever I'm stuck in traffic or forced to wait, I head off on a different path—mental path, that is. My favorite "mind trips" take me right up to heaven. I love thinking about what it will be like when the trumpet toots and we scoot out of here!

Here I am, waiting on hold . . . waiting to speak to a human being . . . waiting for the Lord to return . . . I wonder which will happen first?

May 29

These are the insects you may eat: all kinds of locusts,
winged locusts, crickets, and grasshoppers.
(LEVITICUS 11:22 NCV)

We've come a long way, haven't we, since God gave Moses and Aaron the menu for the Israelites' years in the wilderness? Today some of us have a virtual love affair with food. In fact one expert, the director of an eating disorders center, said, "For many women, loving food has become safer than loving a man. Food never breaks a date, doesn't criticize or reject you." No wonder, then, that when we think of a "gorgeous hunk" these days, the image of a refrigerator comes to mind!

We love to eat—but there's a downside: a big backside! So we go on a diet, but if food is really "safer than loving a man" and, as someone else said, "the closest thing to God," then when we diet we're not just declining another helping of mashed potatoes—we're destroying our whole psyche!

I like to think of banana cream pie as a fruit.

I will perpetuate your memory through all generations;
therefore the nations will praise you for ever and ever.
(PSALM 45:17)

When Bill and I visited Pearl Harbor, we visited the somber memorial to the USS *Arizona*, which sank in 1941 during the surprise air raid that pushed America into World War II. The ship now rests on the bottom of the harbor, a sad monument to the 1,177 men who died when it went down.

A tour guide told us the contents of the great battleship had been left intact and that divers recently were surprised to find, more than fifty years after the disaster, that the sailors' shoes were still there, right where the brave men had died. Some were under the table where the sailors were playing cards. Others were left beside the bunks where they slept or by the ship's signal light where they stood watch. Hearing this description, I couldn't help but think that's the way it will be for us when we fly away to heaven. We won't need earthly shoes there. If the old spiritual hymn is accurate, we'll be walking streets of gold in "dem golden slippers"!

Our final exit **here** *will be our greatest entrance* **there.**

My child, listen to what I say and remember what I command you. Listen carefully to wisdom; set your mind on understanding. . . . Search for it like silver, and hunt for it like hidden treasure. (PROVERBS 2:1–2, 4 NCV)

Things moms would probably never say:

- "How on earth can you see the TV sitting so far back?"

- "Yeah, I used to skip school a lot, too."

- "Just leave all the lights on . . . we have extra money this month for the bill."

- "Let me smell that shirt. Yeah, that's good for another week."

- "Go ahead and keep the stray dog, honey; I'll be glad to take care of it for you."

- "Well, if everybody else's mom says it's okay, that's good enough for me!"

- "I don't have a tissue with me . . . just wipe your nose on your sleeve."

Grandparent: *A thing so simple, even a small child can operate it.*

A cheerful look brings joy to the heart, and good news gives health to the bones. (PROVERBS 15:30)

Celebrate the first of the month by starting a new collection—not of collectibles like stamps or coins or dishes but of "enjoyables"—things that make you laugh. My collection long ago outgrew the Joy Box I first started in a shoebox. Now I have a sixty-by-ten-foot Joy Room attached to our home; it's full of things to make me smile, chuckle, and even guffaw.

When I was going through the really terrible times, I tucked little things like humorous cards and poems and encouraging scriptures in my Joy Box to be enjoyed when I felt blue. Now the walls of my Joy Room are covered with bigger funnies: plaques, pictures, dolls, gadgets, toys, and other happy stuff. One of my favorite laugh makers is Mrs. Beasley, a big, funny-looking doll who seems so realistic, I used to take her with me when I drove to speaking engagements. I loved having Mrs. Beasley along; she's such a good listener!

For every one thing that goes wrong, we have fifty to one hundred blessings!

June 2

Taste and see that the LORD is good. (PSALM 34:8)

At the end of the school year, a kindergarten teacher was receiving gifts from her pupils. The florist's son handed her a gift. She shook it, held it overhead, and said, "I bet I know what it is: some flowers."

"How did you know?" the boy asked.

"Just a wild guess," she answered.

Next the teacher accepted a gift from the sweet-shop owner's daughter, held it overhead, shook it, and said, "I'll bet this is a box of candy."

"How did you know?" the girl asked.

"Oh, just a wild guess," the teacher answered.

The next gift was from the son of the liquor-store owner. The teacher held the package overhead, but it was leaking. She touched a drop with her finger and then touched it to her tongue. "Is it wine?" she asked with a smile. "No-o-o-o-o," the boy replied with some excitement. The teacher repeated the process, taking a larger drop of the leakage to her tongue. "Champagne?" she asked. "No-o-o-o-o-o," the boy replied with even greater excitement.

The teacher took one more taste before declaring, "I give up. What is it?"

With great glee the little boy shouted, "It's a puppy!"

Think about Jesus' example. . . . Do not get tired and stop trying. (HEBREWS 12:3 NCV)

The secret to success is to stay cool and calm on top and paddle like crazy underneath.

We should all live as though someone is writing a book about us.

[Make] the most of every opportunity . . . but understand what the Lord's will is. (EPHESIANS 5:16–17)

Two years after some darling Christian parents found out their son was homosexual, the father wrote to tell me what they'd learned:

> We realized God loved us unconditionally and that He would have that be a model of our love toward our children. . . . When our son recognized that we were not preoccupied with straightening him out, he let down his defenses and freely expressed his love toward us. We weighed the advice of well-meaning friends that we distance ourselves from our child, [but decided that] . . . never does a child need the love and security of his parents more than when . . . dealing with homosexuality. . . . What a terrible time to abandon your child, right when he needs you most!
>
> Today we have a deeper, more loving relationship with him than before. . . . We know the fulfillment that comes from reaching out to others. . . . We've moved from "Why me, Lord?" to "Thank You, Lord!"

We can begin reaching out to others by sharing a smile, an encouraging word, a chance to laugh.

If we confess our sins, he is faithful and just and will
forgive us our sins and purify us from all unrighteousness.
(1 JOHN 1:9)

After my father died, a family friend offered to send me to a well-respected private Christian high school in the South. I was honored to go there.

The strict school's disciplinary system depended on demerits: 150 demerits in one semester, and you went home in disgrace. But right away my roommate and I got *149 demerits* for cooking in our room! (We pilfered some bread and cheese from the cafeteria, used Noxzema face cream as grease, and made grilled-cheese sandwiches by pressing the bread between two irons!)

Knowing we had to get through the entire semester with NO MORE DEMERITS, I sweated out those weeks, scrupulously obeying all the rules, even the signs posted all over the place: GRIPING NOT TOLERATED! Long before Johnny Cash made the song "I Walk the Line" popular, I learned the full meaning of the term— and the overall result was good. I learned to be a positive person, which has helped me deal with stress all my life.

Happiness is homemade.

June 6

*We look to Jehovah our God for his mercy and kindness
just as a servant keeps his eyes upon his master . . . for
the slightest signal.* (PSALM 123:2 TLB)

Even though *millions* of us will be flying away to
meet Jesus in the clouds when the trumpet
sounds, isn't it nice to think there will be no *waiting?*
But until that trumpet blows, we *do* have to wait. And
someone pointed out that God is also experienced at
waiting. When we're struggling through problems
here on earth, trying to cope with the trials that block
our way home, He longingly waits for us to turn to
Him. He watches our stories unfold and waits for us to
acknowledge His plan for our lives. He counts our
tears and waits for us to cry out to Him. God is there
with us wherever we are on the road of life. He is our
comfort today as well as our hope for tomorrow. "This
is a strange journey we walk," one friend wrote to me,
"full of peaks and valleys. But since God is in both
places, *we walk unafraid.*"

*Experience is something you don't get until just after you
need it.*

Peter and the others were very sleepy, but when they awoke fully, they saw the glory of Jesus. (LUKE 9:32 NCV)

A man had just undergone surgery, and as he came out of the anesthesia, he said, "Why are all the blinds drawn, Doctor?"

"There's a big fire across the street, and we didn't want you to wake up and think the operation was a failure."

"Hey, Annette! Put this on! He should be coming to any minute!"

June 8

Then Abraham threw himself down in worship before the Lord, but inside he was laughing in disbelief! "Me, be a father?" he said in amusement. "Me—100 years old? And Sarah, to have a baby at 90?" (GENESIS 17:17 TLB)

This is the time of year when we focus on fathers, those wonderful creatures who traditionally provide the foundation for our families, hold the kid and the mother's purse while she's in the restroom, drive us to the emergency room during crises, and walk our daughters down the aisle when they're married. A good father is a steady rock on a beach of shifting sand and a pillow cushioning life's blows that befall us.

I saw a darling little list somewhere that cited the difference between fathers and single men. Here are two of them:

- Non-fathers drive sports cars that hold the turns. Fathers drive cars that hold the kids.

- Non-fathers fly to Switzerland to go skiing. Fathers drive to Disneyland to ride the Matterhorn.

One little boy defined Father's Day this way: *"Father's Day is just like Mother's Day, only you don't spend as much on a present."*

So a man will leave his father and mother and be united with his wife, and the two will become one body.
(GENESIS 2:24 NCV)

L et's face it. Men are funny. When they're not making us pull our hair out, they're often making us laugh. I remember one time when Bill went down to In-N-Out Burgers, just a block away, to pick up a little treat for us. When he got there, he ordered two hamburgers and two orders of French fries. But when he got the bag home, he started spreading it out and found only one hamburger and one order of fries.

"Oh," he said to me. "That's too bad. I guess they must have forgotten yours!"

I'd go to the end of the earth for Bill. Of course I wouldn't have to if he'd just stop and ask for directions!

June 10

By this all men will know that you are My disciples, if you have love for one another. (JOHN 13:35 NASB)

**D**ear God,
I bet it is very hard for you to love all the people in the world. There are only four people in our family, and I can never do it.
—Nan

A family reunion is the most effective form of birth control.

My people will live in peaceful places and in safe homes and in calm places of rest. (ISAIAH 32:18 NCV)

Except for my Joy Room, which is filled with all sorts of goofy gadgets and funny plaques, my house is pretty well organized—thanks to Bill. If it weren't for the fact that I'm married to this *extremely* organized person (perhaps the only person in the world who *staples* his socks together and hopes for the best before leaving them in my laundry room), my house would be mostly chaos and confusion.

But Bill's anticlutter attitude helps keep me—and all my stuff—in line. Without him, I'd be a first-rate loser. Not that it would be my fault, of course. Things simply have a way of getting away from me. When I turn my back for a mere instant, *poof!* My glasses, pocketbook, keys, and crucial bits of paper bearing absolutely necessary numbers suddenly vanish. It's so remarkable, I expect the phenomenon to be profiled someday on the *X-Files.* The fortunate thing for me, a *loser*, is that, as people often do, I married my opposite—a *finder!*

Those who claim they can take it or leave it probably never had it.

Jesus said, "Come." And Peter left the boat and walked on the water to Jesus. (MATTHEW 14:29 NCV)

**"Oh that? That's so I can keep
your socks paired up in the laundry."**

Men are smartest at fifty—precisely the age when there's nobody in the house who will listen to them.

—BILL VAUGHAN

My mind is filled with apprehension and with gloom.
Oh, restore me soon. Come, O Lord, and make me well.
In your kindness save me. (PSALM 6:3–4 TLB)

For years I've been trying to convince Bill that how you look at life can either bring a sparkle of joy or a handful of gloom. Recently we had car trouble and had to be towed from San Diego to our house nearly a hundred miles away—at a cost of about a dollar per mile. I had never been in a tow truck before, and it was really fun to sit up so high and look down at all the little cars whirring by. But Bill didn't think there was anything cheery about it at all.

Trying to lift his dark and depressing mood, I chirped loudly, "But think of all the gasoline we're saving!" For me, it was a new, fun experience. Why not enjoy ourselves since we had to be doing it anyway? But Bill didn't see it that way. Bill sees the glass half-empty while I see it brimful and running over.

An optimist takes cold water thrown upon his idea, heats it with enthusiasm, and uses the steam to push ahead.

*We also have joy with our troubles, because we know
that these troubles produce patience. And patience
produces character, and character produces hope.*
(ROMANS 5:3–4 NCV)

After putting her children to bed, a mother changed into old slacks and a droopy blouse and then washed her hair in the sink and smeared her face with a slick, green moisturizing cream that hardened into a mask. As she heard the children getting more and more rambunctious, her patience evaporated. At last she threw a towel around her dripping hair and stormed into their room, threatening all sorts of dire punishments if they didn't get back into bed and go to sleep.

As she left the room, she heard a small voice whisper in the darkness, "Who *was* that?"

**The heart of a mother is a deep abyss at the bottom of
which you will always discover forgiveness.**

I want us to help each other with the faith we have. Your faith will help me, and my faith will help you.
(ROMANS 1:12 NCV)

Two are better than one . . . For if they fail, one will scrape the other off the ceiling. (Ecclesiastes 4:9–10, adapted)

We need four hugs a day for survival, eight hugs a day for maintenance, and twelve hugs a day for growth.

—VIRGINIA SATIR

Do you have eyes but fail to see, and ears but fail to hear?
(MARK 8:18)

Sometimes after dads find out about their child's homosexuality, they tend to deny that any problem exists, no matter how glaringly it stares them in the face (in the form of their miserable wives, who feel isolated by their husbands' refusal to talk about it). They're like the man who went on a safari to Africa to photograph elephants. The only problem was that he didn't know what an elephant looked like, so he returned to camp that night totally dejected.

"What's wrong?" someone asked.

"I didn't see a single elephant," the man complained, "just a bunch of huge gray animals with long snouts, big ears, and stringy tails."

The secret to surviving is not in ignoring or denying the problem but in learning to cope with it. Men who come to our Spatula meetings usually aren't happy to be there; they've come at their wives' insistence. It's unusual for them to open up right away. But once they do share a little about their feelings, they feel better— and their marriages improve.

Openness is to wholeness as secrets are to sickness.

Sing to the LORD, all the earth. (1 CHRONICLES 16:23)

Bill is a great husband, but he can't sing. Even so, when the Billy Graham crusade was in our area a few years ago, I signed up both of us to be part of the large choir, because I knew choir members were guaranteed good seats. And because the choir had to be there early, we would avoid the traffic.

During rehearsals I "encouraged" Bill to keep quiet and mouth the words so his lack of singing ability wouldn't be discovered. Everything went well until the crusade began. Then, swept up in all the excitement, Bill joined the thousands of others who lifted joyful voices to heaven. That wouldn't have been a problem except he was carrying a little tape recorder in his shirt pocket so we could enjoy the music and messages again later. That meant he recorded himself loudest of all! And believe me: It WASN'T something you'd want to hear again!

Biblical Characters' Theme Songs

Moses: "There's a Place for Us"; *Noah:* "Raindrops Keep Falling on My Head"; *Lazarus:* "The Second Time Around"; *Peter:* "I'm Sorry"

June 18

The poor will eat and be satisfied; they who seek the
LORD will praise him—may your hearts live forever!
(PSALM 22:26)

There have been times in my life when I didn't worry about my weight; I had plenty of other worries to distract me! But now that Bill and I have settled into our golden years, there are fewer distractions—and more tempting things to eat. Although I don't *think* I'm overeating, and even though I try to be careful about making right choices, somehow, like old age, the extra pounds just seem to magically appear. One day we're a sleek, size 10 glamour girl, and the next thing we know we're the mother of two kids, the grandmother of five, and the final resting place for about ten million fat cells!

That reminds me of a little note sent to me recently by a friend who said, "The beaded belt I wore years ago around my hips is now my necklace, and my rear end looks like an inflated parachute." Still, this darling woman can laugh at these challenges. She said our friendship makes her "fat cells vibrate with laughter."

I'm not fat. I'm calorically gifted!

They were hungry and thirsty, and they were discouraged.
In their misery they cried out to the LORD, and he saved
them from their troubles. (PSALM 107:5 NCV)

Guess what I lost this week...

© 1997 Barbara Johnson

My glasses.

How long must I wrestle with my thoughts and every day have sorrow in my heart? . . . Look on me and answer, O LORD my God. Give light to my eyes, or I will sleep in death. (PSALM 13:2–3)

One of the best descriptions for how an ongoing trial feels came from a lady who told me, "I feel like I've been living in a set of parentheses since I learned that my son's gay. I keep trying to move the parentheses, and they keep stretching out." Whatever you call it, a painful trial is a confining situation. Until God kicks the ends out of your parentheses, you have to handle *today*. Don't deny you're grieving. If you hurt, admit it. As one bumper snicker advises:

WHEN YOU'RE DOWN AND OUT, LIFT UP YOUR HEAD AND SHOUT: "I'M DOWN AND OUT!"

Right now you're raw and hurting, and you have to cling to God's promises even if they don't seem to work for you at the moment. Eventually the pain *will* dilute itself. Then one day you can look around and realize . . . the parentheses are *behind* you!

Even if it burns a little low at times, the secret of life is to always keep the flame of hope alive.

While the earth remains, Seedtime and harvest, / And cold and heat, / And summer and winter, / And day and night / Shall not cease. (GENESIS 8:22 NASB)

Today is the first day of summer, when, as the dictionary explains, "the sun reaches its northernmost point on the celestial sphere" and heads back toward the middle. Perhaps this can be a turning-point day for you, as well, if you've been stuck on the ceiling awhile. Focus today on beginning your trek back to normal. Begin by remembering how much you're loved.

On nights when I can't sleep, I wander out to my Joy Room to find things to lift my spirits. The other night I thought someone else was in the darkened room with me—until I realized it was my own reflection in a special mirror someone sent me. It shows a little boy furtively picking an apple off a tree. Below the picture the sign says, "Look who God loves!"

As I looked into the mirror, I saw myself and thought, *Why, yes, He DOES love me, even when I'm like the little boy and doing things I shouldn't.* I went to bed smiling as I thought of how God loves us all and how He sends His enjoyment to us in unexpected ways.

Earth has no sorrow that heaven cannot heal.

June 22

Be kind and compassionate to one another, forgiving each other, just as in Christ God forgave you. (EPHESIANS 4:32)

A mom named Julia came to our Spatula meeting when her son was in trouble. Later, Julia told me she was being audited by the IRS. She was terrified because she had lied on her tax return, falsely claiming large donations to an orphanage in Mexico—that didn't exist!

I agreed to go with her to the IRS office for moral support. We sat in the car a moment and prayed together. Julia asked the Lord's forgiveness, and I prayed that whoever we talked to would show MERCY. As the tax examiner ushered us into her cubicle I noticed a fish sign on her calendar. Could it BE? Was this lady a Christian? As Julia choked out her confession between tears, the examiner listened intently. Then she reached out, patted Julia on the shoulder, and said, "God forgives you. Now let's see how we can work all this out." And eventually everything *did* work out. Isn't that just like the Lord? When we come to Him in true repentance, He says, "I forgive you. Now let's see what we can do—*together.*"

A Christian does not have to consult his checkbook to see how wealthy she is.

*Keep on working to complete your salvation with fear
and trembling, because God is working in you to help
you want to do and be able to do what pleases him.*
(PHILIPPIANS 2:12–13 NCV)

Paul's message to the Philippians sums up a principle for successful living:

Pray as if everything depended on God, and work
as if everything depended on you.

An old story illustrates this principle. Two frogs were
playing on the rafters of a dairy barn one night and fell
into adjoining pails of cream. Both frogs scrambled for
survival, but one fought longer and harder. When the
farmer came in the next morning, he found one frog
floating on the top of a pail of cream, dead; and the
other frog standing on a cake of butter—exhausted but
happy to be alive.

Moral: When we let problems overwhelm us, when
we stop working to survive, we stop living. But when
we hang in there and fight the good fight we end up
. . . on a cake of butter!

*It's not the pace of life that concerns me. It's the sudden
stop at the end.*

June 24

Jesus . . . cried out in a loud voice, "Lazarus, come out!"
The dead man came out. (JOHN 11:43–44 NCV)

Three friends were talking about death. One of them asked, "When you are in your casket and friends and family are mourning over you, what would you most like to hear them say about you? I've been thinking about it, and I hope they'll say I was one of the great doctors of my time—and a great family man."

The second man said, "I would like to hear them say that I was a loving husband and father, and a devoted schoolteacher who made a difference in shaping the adults of tomorrow."

The third man thought seriously for a moment and then said, "I would like to hear them say . . . 'LOOK! HE'S MOVING! HE'S STILL ALIVE!'"

Church signs I love:

- *Most people want to serve God . . . but only in an advisory capacity.*

- *Wisdom has two parts: (1) Having a lot to say; (2) Not saying it.*

Be beautiful inside, in your hearts, with the lasting charm
of a gentle and quiet spirit which is so precious to God.
(1 PETER 3:4 TLB)

Sometimes I meet people who think I'm a little too joyful—that I'm ducking reality. But I tell them I'm not ignoring the facts—I'm just looking at them and trying to find joy, not misery. There are 365 days in a year, but there's only one day we should be concerned about. Yesterday is a canceled check, and tomorrow is a promissory note. But today is *cash*, ready for us to spend in living. That's why I wake up each morning and rejoice that I can make a fresh start. Nothing has happened, and nobody has goofed it up—we've got another chance!

Johnny had misbehaved and was sent to his room. Later
he emerged and said he had thought it over and said a
prayer. "Fine!" said the pleased mom. "Did you ask God
to help you not misbehave?"

"No," said Johnny. "I asked Him to help you put up
with me!"

June 26

Oh, feed me with your love . . . for I am utterly lovesick.
(Song of Solomon 2:5 tlb)

"My burger's still a little pink on the inside.
Hold the cigarette lighter up to it for a
couple of minutes, would ya?"

Bill says, "Barb cooks for fun, but for food we go out."

With the cross, [God] won the victory and showed the world that they were powerless. (COLOSSIANS 2:15 NCV)

Men, especially those who work in areas such as medicine, mechanics, or engineering, like to deal with things that can be *fixed*. To them, something broken is like a jigsaw puzzle—it looks overwhelming at first, but eventually all the pieces fit together. When parents have a puzzling kid who *can't* or *won't* fit in, these dads are stumped. They can't handle not being able to fix something that's obviously broken.

When a child comes home and says, "Dad, I'm gay," the husband's first instinct is to fix the kid. But in most cases, the kid isn't fixable. Then Dad wants to take *his* turn at that magical sink where parents try to wash their hands of a child. But of course, it doesn't exist.

There will always be a space in every father's heart that's shaped just like his child. But while the heart still loves, the head must recognize that fact I keep repeating to myself and to hurting parents everywhere:

Where there's no control, there's no responsibility.

June 28

No one lights a lamp and hides it! Instead, he puts it on a lampstand to give light to all who enter the room.
(LUKE 11:33 TLB)

One night when Bill wasn't home from work yet, I looked out the window, thankful I could see lights in the neighbors' windows nearby. There is something comforting about lights in the darkness. I think we owe it to passersby to have a light burning in the window—even if it's just a tiny one.

When our son Larry called to say he was disowning us and changing his name, the last words I spoke to him were, "The porch light will always be on for you." A light in the window is like a bright star in the sky; it reminds us someone is waiting to welcome us home. In the movie *Sarah: Plain and Tall,* Sarah was comforted when she saw a tiny light reaching out across the dark Kansas prairie. It showed that she wasn't totally alone. For Christians, there is a beacon that reaches out across the ages, and it is Jesus, the Light of the world.

Dear Lord, prop us up in all our leaning ways.

As for man, his days are like grass, he flourishes like a flower of the field; the wind blows over it and it is gone, and its place remembers it no more. (PSALM 103:15–16)

Think how the westward migration helped settle the United States. First there were only small foot trails through the forests. Eventually the trails were widened to accommodate the pioneers' Conestoga wagons hauling everything from pearls to pump organs—the treasures they would need in their new homes.

But gradually, the pioneers' priorities changed as the days passed and hardships began. Beside a river swollen by flood waters, they discarded the piano that threatened to sink the wagon. At the foot of the mountains, cherished furniture and chests were abandoned. In the middle of the desert, they sometimes left behind the wagon and all it contained. Then, once again, they needed only a narrow trail, one person wide.

That's how we'll approach heaven: empty-handed, with all our "important" earthly priorities littering the roadway behind us as it narrows down to a path just one person wide.

Many folks buy cemetery plots in advance . . . but do nothing about preparing a home in heaven.

June 30

Where your treasure is, there your heart will be also.
(LUKE 12:34)

All we can take with us to heaven is what we leave behind in the lives we touch. A minister's words at a memorial service illustrate this kind of legacy: A woman died shortly after moving to the city where her only child, a woman named Cathy, lived, far from the old hometown. At the memorial service at Cathy's church, the minister said, "I didn't know Cathy's mother. But I know Cathy, and I'm sure I saw her mother in her—just as I know I see Jesus in her. Cathy was her mother's child, and she is Jesus' child. In her life we see the love they both invested in her."

Trust funds can be handed down. Family heirlooms can be passed on. But sooner or later whatever earthly treasures we leave to our loved ones will wind up in that pile of rubble alongside the narrowing pathway to heaven. The only legacy worth anything is our footprints for them to follow . . . right up to God's throne. In the light of eternity, nothing else matters.

Christians **never** *have to say good-bye for the last time.*

Man's steps are ordained by the LORD, / How then can man understand his way? (PROVERBS 20:24 NASB)

Happy first of July! If you're like millions of families, this is the month you travel to vacation sites around the country. Before we started traveling so much ourselves on the Women of Faith tour, we used to have lots of out-of-state guests during the summer. They wanted to stay with us while they visited Disneyland, Knott's Berry Farm, and the other Southern California attractions.

One woman wrote and asked if she could see me while she was in our area seeing the sites, including "Hurts Castle." She was recovering from the depression caused by her two rebellious teenagers, and I guess she didn't know the castle is *Hearst* Castle, not Hurts Castle!

But "Hurts Castle" certainly does describe the place many of us pass through when our kids go haywire. The hurt is there, but we should remember that we're just *visiting* Hurts Castle. We're not becoming permanent residents! Move through the rooms, if you must, but always keep an eye open for the nearest exit!

The journey of a thousand miles . . . begins with wondering if you turned off the iron.

July 2

In my Father's house are many mansions: if it were not so, I would have told you. I go to prepare a place for you. (JOHN 14:2 KJV)

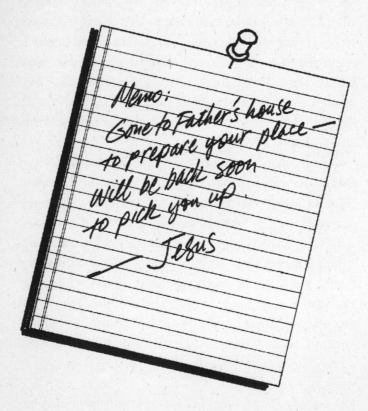

Memo:
Gone to Father's house
to prepare your place —
will be back soon
to pick you up.

— Jesus

And if I go and prepare a place for you, I will come again, and receive you unto myself, that where I am, there ye may be also. (JOHN 14:3 KJV)

Lord,
while you're
busy preparing
a place for me,
prepare me,
as well,
for that place!
— Bart

July 4

Then you will know the truth, and the truth will make you free. (JOHN 8:32 NCV)

Celebrate the birthday of our nation's freedom by liberating yourself from the misery that imprisons you from dealing with a wayward child. Remember: Pain may be inevitable, but *misery* is *optional!* Three principles open that prison door:

- Love your child unconditionally.
- Let your child go—release him to God's care.
- Pray constantly!

We may not love what our children are doing, but we love *THEM.* However, one person's sin can't be allowed to destroy everyone else. When your child is in trouble, the main thing is to keep your relationship with God and your spouse and family solid while continuing to reach out to the wandering child. You may have to tell an adult child, "I can't let you destroy the family. I'll help you find another place."

Then pray. Just as you once covered up your little one's shoulders when you tucked him in at night, now you cover him constantly in prayer.

Each day God gives us grace . . . for the next step.

You are God's children whom he loves, so try to be like him. (EPHESIANS 5:1 NCV)

s I love and encourage others . . . as I lift up Jesus,

> I serve Jesus,
> I imitate Jesus,
> I, too, am blessed.

Priceless gift to give for free: *The gift of a prayer. Let your friends and loved ones know you pray for them—and then do it!*

July 6

Worship the Lord with the beauty of holy lives.
(PSALM 96:9 TLB)

No matter how old I get, I don't want to be thought of as elderly! Instead, I want to be like the patients of the plastic surgeon who said, "There is no such thing as an old woman! My patients are not vain. They only want to let the little girl out!"

That's me, all right! I'm NOT old; I'm just a mature little girl. And I have a little something extra, now that I'm heading toward the sunset. Unfortunately, that little something extra is often in the worst possible place. I love the little quip that says:

> With age a woman gains wisdom, maturity, self-assurance . . . and ten pounds right on the hips.

I often say, "Actually, my body's a perfect ten under here. I just keep it covered with fat so it won't get scratched!" For many of us, that perfect-ten body is attached to a thirty-year-old mind in an antique display case! But who cares? Celebrate youth—no matter how many decades you've been youthful!

You know you're getting older . . . when "happy hour" is a nap!

The good man does not escape all troubles—he has them too. But the Lord helps him in each and every one.
(PSALM 34:19 TLB)

Jesus knows how you feel when you're hurt, scared, and alone. And He's always with you to wrap you in His comfort blanket of love. But maybe right now you're in such a state of shock that you can't accept that promise.

Maybe you're like the little boy who was afraid of the dark and wanted his mother to stay in the room with him at bedtime.

"Son, I can't see why you're so afraid of the dark. Don't you know God is with you?" the mother asked.

"Yes, I know that," the boy replied, "but I want someone with skin on."

If you need "someone with skin on" right now, I know just how you feel. I've got lots of skin—too much, judging by my looks. But I always remember this important rule of life: You're not old unless you get wrinkles in your HEART!

A little boy's prayer: *Dear God, take care of the whole world. And please, God, take care of Yourself, or we're all sunk!*

July 8

*When they were discouraged, I smiled and that
encouraged them and lightened their spirits.*
(JOB 29:24 TLB)

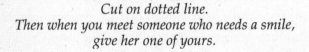

*Cut on dotted line.
Then when you meet someone who needs a smile,
give her one of yours.*

Bumper Snicker: *Cheer up! Someday you'll be dead!*

You have been saved by grace through believing. You did not save yourselves; it was a gift from God. (EPHESIANS 2:8 NCV)

The foundation of all joy for Christians is that we can live as though Christ died yesterday, rose today, and is coming tomorrow. Joy starts here, and it's for everyone—no strings, no admission fee, because we are saved by grace and grace alone. That's what the apostle Paul meant when he said we are "saved by grace through believing." It doesn't have anything to do with what we can do. As I always say:

JUSTICE IS WHEN WE GET WHAT WE DESERVE.

MERCY IS WHEN WE DON'T GET WHAT WE DESERVE.

BUT GRACE IS WHEN WE GET WHAT WE *DON'T* DESERVE.

Grace is God's unmerited favor that is showered upon us. And that grace is FREE to all who ask for it. We begin by trusting Jesus Christ. He's our first experience of joy. And we continue to have splashes of joy as we learn to trust in Him alone.

Psalm 23 (abbreviated version): *The Lord is my Shepherd . . . and that's all I need to know.*

July 10

We are hard pressed on every side, but not crushed;
perplexed, but not in despair; persecuted, but not
abandoned; struck down, but not destroyed.
(2 CORINTHIANS 4:8–9)

The difference between winning and losing is how we react to disappointments. Some of us remember in living color the day a spouse walked out or a rebellious child left home. Others have felt the twisting knife of grief when a loved one dies, and many know the sinking feeling when the doctor says, "I'm sorry. It's malignant." One woman described how she chose to react on the day her job was eliminated:

> When I was called into the meeting where I would later be fired . . . I grabbed a pad and wrote with a purple highlighter "Pain Is Inevitable But Misery Is Optional!" I took the pad with me into the meeting and continued to glance at the words and repeat them in my head. It was the only thing that helped me keep my place and my dignity through . . . one of the most humiliating moments of my life.

This woman knew: *Losers let stress turn life into something bad, but winners turn stress into something good.*

LORD, show your love to us as we put our hope in you.
(PSALM 33:22 NCV)

The Reverend Bruce Larson once visited the Menninger Foundation, one of the world's leading psychiatric institutions. He asked staff members, "What is the single most important ingredient in your treatment here?"

The doctors answered, "We know it's hope. We don't know how it comes or how to give it to people, but we know that when people get hope, they get well."

"What does hope look like?" Larson asked.

These skilled medical doctors told him they could tell almost immediately when patients suddenly turned the corner and realized they did not have to go on as they had before. As Larson put it in a message he preached: *Hope means you are no longer a prisoner of your track record.*

I get letters from folks who have learned the meaning of hope. Their track record may sound depressing, but they know they are not prisoners. Instead they are free, because hope set them free.

Madness takes its toll. Please have exact change.

July 12

We love because he first loved us. (1 JOHN 4:19)

To those who know how to love and be loved, marriage is life's greatest bargain. When spouses can be best friends, the bargain includes a bonus. Love can be fresh for couples who learn how to give each other solid emotional support through the years.

Marriage starts off with a treasure chest of gold— the love each partner feels for the other. Every act of devotion puts more love into the marital strong box. Every unloving act takes some out. When the treasure box is full, we live on a high note of secure confidence, and spouses are able to make rich exchanges of sentiment. But when the treasury is empty, life is a bankrupt procession of empty days.

Yes, we all have tense times, but being part of a warm, supportive family reminds us:

The best things in life aren't things.

How can you say to your brother, "Brother, let me take the speck out of your eye," when you yourself fail to see the plank in your own eye? (LUKE 6:42)

Appreciation is a kindling force. When we truly appreciate folks, we see them in a completely new light. Whole libraries have been written about the family, but I think the entire subject could be put into one statement:

The only way to live happily with folks is to overlook their faults and admire their virtues.

You can't change people, so why not enjoy the good parts? A clear definition of love could be: "practicing the art of appreciation." The poet Robert Browning said, "Take away love and this earth is a tomb." And the medical doctor William Menninger repeatedly said, "Love is the medicine for most of mankind's ills." It's also the medicine for most of our personal ills.

A boy took his baby sister fishing while his parents went shopping. "I'll never do that again!" he told his parents that evening. "I didn't catch a thing!"

"Was she too noisy?" asked the mother.

"It wasn't that," the boy said. "She ate all the bait."

July 14

*The trumpet will sound, and those who have died will
be raised to live forever, and we will all be changed.*
(1 CORINTHIANS 15:52 NCV)

It's downright fun to think about the inheritances
awaiting us in heaven, but there's one thing that
makes me positively giddy. It's the new body I'll have
instantly when the Rapture is complete.

Now, the Bible doesn't say anywhere that we get to
choose what kind of new body we get, but it's fun to
pretend we'll be able to pick and choose specific body
parts in heaven. Let's see . . . I might ask for a dynamic
voice like Billy Graham's, a caring heart like Mother
Teresa's, and tireless feet like John the Baptist's. Maybe
I'll request the patience of Job, the artistic ability of
Michelangelo, the wisdom of Solomon, the insight of
C. S. Lewis, and hands like Noah's—or perhaps hands
like the Master Carpenter's . . .

Classified Ad
*For Sale: Antique desk suitable for lady with thick legs
and large drawers.*

Seek first his kingdom and his righteousness, and all these things will be given to you as well. (MATTHEW 6:33)

For attractive lips, speak words of kindness.
For lovely eyes, seek out the good in people.
For a slim figure, share your food with the hungry.
For beautiful hair, let a child run his fingers
      through it once a day.
For poise, walk with the knowledge that you'll
      never walk alone. —SAM LEVENSON

"If only I were as young as my mirror thinks I am!"

July 16

For he orders his angels to protect you wherever you go.
(PSALM 91:11 TLB)

Many years ago, two children fell into the river above Niagara Falls during a boating accident. The boat operator was killed, and a seven-year-old boy was swept over the falls but miraculously survived. His little sister was near the brink of the falls when a tourist spotted her. He climbed over the guardrail, stepped into the water, and reached out over the murderous current for the child. At the last possible moment, the little girl grasped his thumb. But the additional weight added to his precarious position caused the rescuer to lose his balance and wobble dangerously close to the precipice. He called for help, and a second tourist climbed the rail and helped both the man and the child back to shore. The rescuers were just two "ordinary" men, two tourists. And it might be that they simply found extra adrenaline that day to pull the little girl back from plummeting over the falls. But many who saw them risk their lives for a stranger compared them with angels.

An angel is someone who brings out the angel in you.

Anything that is old and worn out is ready to disappear.
(HEBREWS 8:13 NCV)

On her eightieth birthday, Abigail Van Buren was asked to name her biggest accomplishment. She answered succinctly, "Surviving!" Then she shared her advice for aging gracefully: "Fear less; hope more. Eat less; chew more. Talk less; say more. Hate less; love more. And never underestimate the power of forgiveness."

Her thoughts remind me of the elderly couple who took a memory-enhancement course. Later they met their friend Bill on the street, and the husband said to him, "Bill, you just have to take this incredible course we just finished. It's fantastic!"

Bill said, "What's the name of the course?"

The husband turned to his wife and asked, "What's that flower? You know, the one with the long stem and the thorns?"

"You mean a rose?" his wife replied.

"Yeah, that's it! (pause . . .) Rose, what was the name of that memory course?"

A benefit of growing older: *There's nothing left to learn the hard way.*

July 18

The angel said to him: "Do not be afraid, Zechariah; your prayer has been heard. Your wife Elizabeth will bear you a son, and you are to give him the name John. He will be a joy and delight to you, and many will rejoice because of his birth." . . . Zechariah asked the angel, "How can I be sure of this? I am an old man and my wife is well along in years." The angel answered, "I am Gabriel. I stand in the presence of God, and I have been sent to speak to you and to tell you this good news." (LUKE 1:13–14, 18–19)

Setting a good example for children takes all the fun out of middle age. —WILLIAM FEATHER

Do not forget to entertain strangers, for by so doing some people have entertained angels without knowing it.
(HEBREWS 13:2)

Just as the Bible instructs us to "entertain strangers" because they might be angels in disguise, we should also be ready to *rescue* strangers if God decides to use *us* in angelic ways. Most of us probably hope He won't send us out to lean over the edge of a precipice and pull someone back from the brink of death. Instead He might send us to, say, Omaha—assigned to the airplane seat next to a brokenhearted mother or a hardhearted father. It could be someone who's trying to run away from God.

Or He might plant us in a crowd where one person, quietly standing up for what's right, could make all the difference. He might send us to a hospital or a prison or a nursing home to be the loving hands of Jesus. Or He might just put us in the grocery-store checkout line of a weary clerk who hasn't heard a kind word all afternoon. Opportunities to do good are everywhere, but they're sometimes fleeting. Don't miss a chance to be angelic!

People with a heart for God have a heart for people.

July 20

No wonder we are happy in the Lord! For we are trusting him. (PSALM 33:21 TLB)

My friend Marilyn Meberg says that many of us take ourselves too seriously. We worry about always looking good, correct, and dignified. The result is that we miss out on a lot of fun.

"There are many, many times in your daily experience when you can turn your situation around and laugh," Marilyn said. "Laugh at the situation. Laugh at yourself. When you do, you're in charge instead of it being in charge of you."

Marilyn's advice reminds me of the adage that says, "Humor is God's weapon against worry, anxiety, and fear." Laughing people can survive and land on their feet, because laughter helps us love one another. Those who cannot laugh will stay in the cesspool of despair. Remember: Your day goes the way the corners of your mouth turn.

Happy is the woman who can laugh at herself; she will never cease to be amused.

May the God of your fathers, the Almighty, bless you
with blessings of heaven above and of the earth beneath . . .
blessings of the grain and flowers, blessings reaching
to the utmost bounds of the everlasting hills.
(Genesis 49:25–26 TLB)

Can you just "Stick a Geranium in Your Hat and Be Happy"? I know you can, no matter what happens. We all have to endure troubles in life. Sometimes we may go along for a while with just common irritations and then, WHAM! A big problem hits, and we have a real valley experience. But I believe that you grow in the valleys because that's where all the fertilizer is. We can choose to gather to our hearts the thorns of disappointment, failure, loneliness, and dismay due to our present situations, or we can gather the flowers of God's grace, boundless love, abiding presence, and unmatched joy. I choose to gather the flowers, and I hope you will too.

There are times, regardless of the score, when just being ALIVE is to be winning.

*In everything we do we try to show that we are true
ministers of God. We patiently endure suffering and
hardship and trouble of every kind.*
(2 CORINTHIANS 6:4 TLB)

Christianity is more than a storm cellar; it is a way of life.

Rebuke a wise man and he will love you. Instruct a wise man and he will be wiser still; teach a righteous man and he will add to his learning. (PROVERBS 9:8–9)

Men are wonderful creatures; they truly are. They compliment us—and complement us! They can make us cry; they can build us up—or leave us flattened. They support us and nurture us and console us. In short, they're nice to have around! But one of their most valuable gifts to us women, in my rather lopsided opinion at least, is that they give us so much to laugh about. Here are some of my favorite quips and jokes about men.

- Men don't really lose their hair—it just goes underground and comes out their ears!

- Morning memory jog: *First the pants, THEN the shoes.*

- Lewis and Clark were not really meant to explore the West for all those months. They simply did not want to admit in front of Sacajawea that they were lost.

- In buying a gift for your wife, practicality can be more expensive than extravagance. —MAX LUCADO

Mixed Maxim: *He who laughs first will be last.*

July 24

Let this encourage God's people to endure patiently every trial and persecution, for they are his saints who remain firm to the end in obedience to his commands and trust in Jesus. (REVELATION 14:12 TLB)

Age is the great leveler when it comes to coping with advancing technology. It used to be when we women couldn't figure out how to run some gadget, we could call our husbands and they'd press a few buttons and send us on our way. But that's changing.

Now things are so complicated some husbands can't figure them out, either. One woman told me her husband bought a new large-screen, picture-within-the-picture television that came with a *sixty-four-page* instruction manual. (And we know what he did with that, right? Used it as a coaster.) The woman said, "By trial and error, he learned how to turn it on and change the channel—and didn't even attempt to learn the zillions of other things this monster can do." Technology is pushing us to do everything faster on life's highway—just when most of us would be content to pull over and snooze along the shoulder.

Modern Maxim: *For every action there is an equal and opposite criticism.*

Even we Christians . . . also groan to be released from pain and suffering. We, too, wait anxiously for that day when God will give us our full rights as his children, including the new bodies he has promised us—bodies that will never be sick again and will never die.
(ROMANS 8:23 TLB)

I love thinking about trading in my worn-out earthly body for a new heavenly model. Joni Eareckson Tada, in her book *Heaven . . . Your Real Home*, compares this attitude with the enthusiasm her horse used to feel when she was headed home:

> My weary mount would be wet with sweat, her head hanging low. . . . Then as soon as she caught a whiff of home . . . her ears would pick up and her pace would quicken. . . . After a quick unsaddling, she would joyfully roll in the dirt and take long, deep drinks from the trough. How good it feels for a beast to be home, to be able to rest. How good it will feel for us to rest, to be at home.

The three stages of life: *youth, maturity, and "My, you're looking good!"*

Give thanks to the LORD, for His lovingkindness is everlasting. (2 CHRONICLES 20:21 NASB)

While support groups can be godsends to hurting parents, there's really no substitute for that one dedicated friend who loves you no matter how miserable you are and no matter how hard you are to be with! Just imagine how comforting it would be to have a friend who would listen to you pour out your feelings of being "terrified of the future," as one mother of an AIDS victim wrote. Or to listen to another mother express "fear for my son, terror for his eternal destination, and my grief for what seems lost."

What an honor—and a blessing—it would be to reach out to a friend in that way to pull that person back from the brink of despair. If you can be a friend like this, you are a lifeline—a tool used by God to bring His love to an otherwise hopeless situation. But God's "tool" is also blessed by the kindnesses bestowed because:

A kindness done is never lost. It may take awhile, but like a suitcase on a luggage carousel, it will return again. —H. JACKSON BROWN

*Then the righteous will answer him, "Lord, when did
we see you hungry and feed you, or thirsty and give you
something to drink? When did we see you a stranger and
invite you in, or needing clothes and clothe you? When
did we see you sick or in prison and go to visit you?"
The King will reply, ". . . Whatever you did for one of
the least of these brothers of mine, you did for me."*
(MATTHEW 25:37–40)

If you're refusing to budge from your cesspool when
a friend is inviting you to leave, you're not only
denying a gift for yourself, you may also be depriving
the friend of a much-needed blessing as well.

For some people, it's extremely difficult to accept
help. They're afraid that by accepting assistance they
will become obligated or indebted to that person, and
they don't like owing anything to anyone! But what
they don't realize is that by refusing help, they are
stripping that person of something good. So even
when you'd rather stand alone . . .

*In your grief, go limp, and let others carry you for a
while. In doing so, you'll make a friend!*

The memory of the righteous will be a blessing.
(PROVERBS 10:7)

A reporter was visiting an elderly couple who had just celebrated their sixty-fifth wedding anniversary. He was touched by the way the husband continually spoke to his wife in terms of endearment, always calling her "Sweetheart," "Honey," or "Dear."

"It's so sweet, the way you address your wife in those endearing ways," the reporter said to the husband.

"Well, to tell you the truth," the old man answered, "I forgot her name about ten years ago."

* * *

As an aircraft landed at the airport, a flight attendant made this announcement:

Ladies and gentlemen, we have a very special person on board this evening. He is ninety-six years old today, and this is his very first flight. As you deplane this evening, please stop by the cockpit and wish our captain Happy Birthday!

It is easier to get older than wiser.

A real friend will be more loyal than a brother.
(PROVERBS 18:24 NCV)

If you're going to encourage other folks, the best place to start is with yourself. Collect only "life-lifters" and discard all the "life-sinkers."

If you look hard enough, you can see the positive and even humorous side of anything. One lady who faced surgery for breast cancer found a creative way to do that. Before she was wheeled into the operating room, she donned a propeller beanie on her head and a large, colorful sign on her chest. The sign said, "GIVE IT YOUR BEST SHOT!"

In the operating room, a nurse saw the sign and asked her what it meant. She smiled and replied, "Well, when that surgeon cuts on me today, I just want him to be in a REAL GOOD MOOD!"

With a positive attitude, tears of sorrow will start to glisten with gladness. In fact, tears bring the rainbows into our lives that lead to pots of joy.

Enjoy the little things. One day you may look back and realize . . . they were the big things.

July 30

As the elect of God, holy and beloved, put on tender
mercies, kindness, humility, meekness, longsuffering;
bearing with one another, and forgiving one another. . . .
But above all these things put on love.
(COLOSSIANS 3:12–14 NKJV)

My friend Darcey Hripak sent me a beautiful little story that endearingly illustrates the wardrobe Paul describes. My favorite garments are the tender mercies, depicted as "the underwear of God's wardrobe—personal and  next to the skin," and longsuffering: "Sometimes I wish that old rag would just wear out so I could get something more glamorous and colorful. But I know God has fashioned even this to enhance my life."

And I adore the way Darcey illustrates love. She says, "You might think of love as your best hat. . . . It is that one essential accessory you should never leave behind. Never go anywhere without love!"

Overheard in a women's fitting room: *"They don't make large as big as they used to!"*

He has sent me to bind up the brokenhearted, . . . to comfort all who mourn, . . . to bestow on them a crown of beauty instead of ashes, the oil of gladness instead of mourning, and a garment of praise instead of a spirit of despair. (ISAIAH 61:1–3)

Being thankful is like an analogy I once read that talks of being given a dish of sand and being told there were particles of iron in it. We could look for the iron by sifting our clumsy fingers through the sand, but we wouldn't find much. If we took a magnet, however, and pulled it through the sand, it would draw to itself the almost invisible iron particles. The unthankful heart, like the clumsy fingers, discovers no mercies, but let the thankful heart sweep through the day, and as the magnet finds the iron, so will the thankful heart find heavenly blessings every time!

If we thanked God for all the good things, we wouldn't have time to complain about the bad.

August 1

Keep yourselves in God's love as you wait for the mercy of our Lord Jesus Christ to bring you to eternal life.
(JUDE 21)

Celebrate the first of August by doing as little as possible! August is a time of heat and lethargy. The summer vacations are usually over. The company has gone home. And there aren't any holidays (except in those areas where schools start in August—then parents have a holiday from minute-by-minute child-tending! I love that commercial that shows a parent skipping down the store aisles, collecting back-to-school supplies and singing what we usually think of as a Christmas song: "It's the MOST wonderful time of the year!").

Find a nice, comfy spot—a hammock under the trees or a couch under the air conditioner—and focus on funny things. Take a tour of your Joy Box and enjoy the laugh getters you've collected. Or rent some funny videos and treat yourself to a laugh fest. It takes forty-three muscles to frown but only seventeen to smile. So, in the August heat, conserve energy. Turn off your worries and troubles and turn on your smile!

Sometimes, having a good day can be as easy as choosing to have one.

Be joyful always; pray continually; give thanks in all circumstances, for this is God's will for you in Christ Jesus. (1 THESSALONIANS 5:16–18)

A friend wrote to me, saying, "There is NOTHING like a deep, gut-stirring, tear-streaming laugh." Lots of experts agree. They say laughter helps control pain in four ways: (1) by distracting attention, (2) by reducing tension, (3) by changing expectations, and (4) by increasing the production of endorphins, the body's natural painkillers.

When you laugh, it takes your mind off the pain and actually creates a degree of anesthesia. Laughter reduces muscle tension and has even been known to have the same effect on a headache as aspirin or other pain relievers. It changes our expectations by changing our attitudes. Laughter is a shock absorber that eases the blows of life. So . . . let's laugh!

Church signs that make me smile:

- *God loves everyone but probably prefers "fruits of the spirit" over "religious nuts"!*

- *God grades on the cross, not on the curve.*

- *Exposure to the Son may prevent burning!*

- *For all you do, His blood's for YOU!*

August 3

Eye has not seen, nor ear heard, / Nor have entered into the heart of man / The things which God has prepared for those who love Him. (1 CORINTHIANS 2:9 NKJV)

After our son Tim was killed by a drunk driver in Canada, I identified his body in the same mortuary where, five years earlier *to the day*, I had identified Steve's body after he was killed in Vietnam. As I stood there, looking at another boy in a box, grief rolled over me until I thought I would drown.

But when I left the mortuary on that hot August day, I experienced a thrilling "frozen picture" of Tim in heaven. I looked up, and there in the sky was Tim's smiling face! He was surrounded with a bright, shining light, and I heard him say, "Don't cry, Mom! I'm not there. I'm rejoicing around the throne of God."

Miraculous experiences aren't familiar to me. I'd never had one before and haven't had one since. But perhaps God knew I needed something extra that day. If you're drowning in grief, ask God to give *you* a frozen picture of your loved one in heaven so that you, too, can know peace.

Earth has no sorrow that heaven cannot heal.
—THOMAS MOORE

The created world itself can hardly wait for what's coming next. Everything in creation is being more or less held back. God reins it in until both creation and all the creatures are ready and can be released at the same moment into the glorious times ahead. Meanwhile, the joyful anticipation deepens. (ROMANS 8:19–21 TM)

"I'm getting so old that all my friends in heaven will think I didn't make it."

Reprinted from *Church Is Stranger Than Fiction* by Mary Chambers. © 1990 by Mary Chambers. Used by permission of InterVarsity Press, P.O. Box 1400, Downers Grove, Illinois 60515.

August 5

John continued to preach the Good News, saying many other things to encourage the people. (LUKE 3:18 NCV)

When something is restored it pops backs in place, like an out-of-joint bone that is popped back into alignment, relieving the pain. Encouragement works like an emotional chiropractor—and both "doctor" and patient benefit from the treatment. Share a word of encouragement today and enjoy a boomerang blessing. Here are some ideas:

- Leave a note on your mailbox, encouraging your mail carrier by saying he or she "carries the mail with class."

- Tell the person in front of you in line at the grocery store that you love the gentle way she speaks to her kids.

- Tell your daughter she's an awesome child of God . . . as well as a superb athlete, student, friend, or youth group leader.

- Tuck a note into your husband's briefcase that says, "I thank God for you each day!"

Sympathy says, "I'm sorry." Compassion says, "I'll help."

The LORD is good to those who hope in him, to those who seek him. (LAMENTATIONS 3:25 NCV)

The boss urgently needed to speak to one of his employees on a Saturday. He called the man's home and a child answered a whispered, "Hello?"

"Is your daddy home?" the boss asked.

"Yes," whispered the small voice.

"May I speak to him?" the boss asked.

"No," the kid replied.

Perplexed, the boss asked to speak to the child's mother and got the same reply. "Well, are there any other adults there?" he asked.

"Yes," the child said, "a policeman and a fireman."

"There's a policeman *and* a fireman there?" The boss was getting worried. "Well, may I speak to one of the adults?"

"No, they're busy," the child whispered.

"Busy doing what?" the boss asked.

With a muffled giggle the child replied, "They're looking for *me!*"

Even though children are deductible, they can also be taxing. —NELSON'S BIG BOOK OF LAUGHTER

August 7

Good men long to help each other. (PROVERBS 12:12 TLB)

When our relationship with our son Larry was restored after an eleven-year estrangement, he and I taped an interview so we could share what we had learned from our trial. I told Larry how wonderful it is that we don't have to live in bondage to the unhappy memories of the past. "That's because we've been able to forgive each other," Larry replied. "Forgiveness is a very powerful thing—the ability to forgive and the ability to be forgiven. When someone comes to you and says, 'I was wrong in what I did to you. Will you forgive me?' that's a very powerful thing . . . because it releases a burden of guilt."

Larry recalled how our own relationship had nearly been destroyed when I first learned of his homosexuality. "Some of the things that you said were terrible," he remembered, "reckless words, like a piercing sword."

I remembered. That's why today I tell people to shove a sock in their mouths, or they'll say the wrong thing in their current state of panic.

Life can be only understood backward, but it must be lived forward.

A woman by the name of Martha welcomed [Jesus] and made him feel quite at home. She had a sister, Mary, who sat before the Master, hanging on every word he said. But Martha was pulled away by all she had to do in the kitchen. Later, she stepped in, interrupting them. "Master, don't you care that my sister has abandoned the kitchen to me? Tell her to lend me a hand."

The Master said, "Martha, dear Martha, you're fussing far too much and getting yourself worked up over nothing. One thing only is essential, and Mary has chosen it—it's the main course, and won't be taken from her." (LUKE 10:38–42 TM)

Are you preoccupied with folding the napkins while the main course is being served in the next room? Are you indulging in tears of loneliness while friends and loved ones are calling you to come with them? Are you too busy assembling the church newsletter in the office to slip into the sanctuary and pray? Too wrapped up in preparing your Sunday school handouts to find a few quiet moments to read God's Word?

One thing only is essential. Got it?

The main thing is to keep the main thing the main thing!

August 9

Continue praying, keeping alert, and always thanking God. . . . Pray that I can speak in a way that will make it clear. (COLOSSIANS 4:2, 4 NCV)

As I started toward the podium to speak at a conference, a lady grabbed my arm and said, "Don't step back too far because there's a hole in the carpet, and you'll catch your heel in it." I continued toward the platform, but another lady stopped me and whispered, "Don't push on the podium. The flowers may fall over!" By the time I got to the podium, I was already stressed out. But just as I began to speak, a maintenance man slipped onto the stage carrying a glass of water. *How nice!* I thought. *Finally something positive.* But as he set the glass on the podium, he said, "Be careful. The last speaker spilled her water into the microphone and almost electrocuted herself."

I managed to get through the talk without triggering calamity. But I had to laugh later when someone said, "Barb, you seem so relaxed and happy, as though you have no stress in your life at all!"

Of all the things I've lost, I miss my mind the most.

I praise the LORD because he advises me. Even at night, I feel his leading. (PSALM 16:7 NCV)

God sometimes uses the smallest gestures of kindness to touch a life of torment, ease a broken heart, or light a spark of hope. I see this happen at my book table when we give away the flat, iridescent marbles I call "splashes of joy." We say, "Put it on your window sill. When it sparkles it reminds you of all your blessings."

Then we go home, and inevitably the letters arrive. One woman said she gave the marble to her sister, who was battling breast cancer. The sister had her daughter buy some similar flat marbles so she could give them to doctors, nurses, and other hospital staffers. "They won't forget her," her sister wrote, "or the joy she infused them with!"

When she died at the age of forty-five, bowls full of splashes of joy were placed around the church at her funeral, and everyone was invited to take some home. And some of those people will, in turn, pass along that little bit of joy to someone else . . .

Each of us can decrease the suffering of the world by adding to its joy.

My eyes pour out tears to God. (Job 16:20 NCV)

At one time or another, *everybody* cries. The Old Testament tells us that David wept on several occasions. Jesus cried when He learned His friend Lazarus had died. He also wept over the city of Jerusalem and its inhabitants.

For years, I've urged grieving parents to *schedule* regular private times to pour out their grief in tears. Now researchers are finding that people who cry enjoy better health overall. It seems that healthy people view tears positively while those who are plagued with illnesses see tears as unnecessary, even humiliating.

Medical students and even practicing MDs are urged not to give tranquilizers to weeping patients too soon but to let tears do their own therapeutic work. Laughter and tears are natural medicines. They both allow us to reduce stress and let out our negative feelings so we can recharge. Think of tears as one of the body's best natural resources.

These medical experts are just now catching on to what poets have known for centuries. As Shakespeare put it:

> **To weep is to make less the depth of grief.**
> —KING HENRY VI

You build your room above the clouds. You make the clouds your chariot, and you ride on the wings of the wind. (PSALM 104:3 NCV)

Several years ago when my doctor insisted I start exercising, I came up with the perfect solution. I try to respond to as much of my mail as possible with a phone call instead of a letter. That's lots of phone calls! But while I'm on the phone, I'm also on the exercise bike Bill set up for me in my Joy Room.

As I pedal and talk, I also enjoy all the goofy things in the Joy Room. And while I ride, I also tour the country, making imaginary cross-country trips along a big, colored map of the United States on the wall by the bike. A pushpin goes into the map every twenty-five miles so I can keep track of the accumulated miles. I try to ride ten to fifteen miles every day we're home. And in between phone calls I pray for my friends along the route! Riding, talking, touring, and praying—with this multiple workout, I'll be a size 4 in no time!

I've reached that point in life where about all I can exercise is CAUTION!

August 13

How priceless is your unfailing love! Both high and low among men find refuge in the shadow of your wings. They feast on the abundance of your house; you give them drink from your river of delights. (PSALM 36:7–8)

Just as you received Christ Jesus as Lord, continue to live in him, rooted and built up in him, strengthened in the faith as you were taught, and overflowing with thankfulness. (COLOSSIANS 2:6–7)

Loving a child unconditionally is a beautiful idea, but it is far beyond human strength. After God brought about a restoration between our son Larry and us, I asked him, "How do you think unconditional love worked in the years you weren't in touch with us?"

He answered, "I think that's when the parent has to turn it all over to God. Scripture says, 'The king's heart is in the hand of the LORD, / Like the rivers of water; He turns it wherever He wishes' (Proverbs 21:1 NKJV). This tells me God turns people's hearts wherever He wants them to go. You've just got to trust God and know He will touch their hearts at the right time."

Truly, no one can love unconditionally in his or her own strength. You must trust God to turn the heart of your wayward child (and to keep your own heart turned the right way, as well).

Instead of showing someone the gate, try mending the fence.

August 15

Peter was sleeping, bound with two chains between two soldiers; and the guards before the door were keeping the prison. Now behold, an angel of the Lord stood by him . . . he struck Peter on the side and raised him up, saying, "Arise quickly!" And his chains fell off his hands.
(ACTS 12:6–7 NKJV)

Sue, a volunteer, hurried inside the school's huge walk-in freezer to retrieve two bags of ice for the thirsty kids in the school's annual field day. No one was in the kitchen when she opened the massive, six-inch-thick door of the freezer and stepped inside. She found the ice and turned toward the door.

"My heart stopped," she said. "There was no door handle! It was just a big, smooth, metal slab set into the wall. I immediately exploded into full-bore panic." She screamed at the top of her lungs, and suddenly the door opened. The custodian stood before her. He smiled and said, "It's a swinging door. Just push."

When hurting parents feel frozen in "full-bore panic," what a blessing it is to have someone show them a simple way out of their misery.

What do you get when you cross a snowman with a vampire? Frostbite!

Finally, all of you should be in agreement, understanding each other, loving each other as family, being kind and humble. (1 PETER 3:8 NCV)

Isolation is what sinks hurting parents—especially mothers, but we *don't* have to suffer alone. We must push back the curtain of isolation and realize we are NOT alone—ever! When it feels as if no one can understand your torment, remember God's promise to Isaiah—and to all His children ever since then:

Do not fear, for I am with you; Do not be dismayed, for I am your God. I will strengthen you and help you; I will uphold you with my righteous right hand. (Isaiah 41:10)

We need to keep repeating this promise until it totally *marinates* our spirits. One woman said she does this by taping encouraging verses like Isaiah 41:10 to the refrigerator door. "When our children share stuff my husband and I wish we didn't know, we go to our refrigerator door and read the reminders that our boys belong to God—He controls their destiny."

To live in hearts we leave behind . . . is not to die.
—THOMAS CAMPBELL

August 17

They blessed Rebekah and said, "Our sister, may you be the mother of thousands of people. . . ."
(GENESIS 24:60 NCV)

An old country doctor went way out into the boonies to deliver a baby. It was so far out, there was no electricity. When the doctor arrived, no one was home except for the laboring mother and her five-year-old son. The doctor instructed the child to hold a lantern high so he could see to deliver the baby. The child held the lantern, the mother pushed, and after a while, the doctor lifted the newborn baby by the feet and swatted him on the bottom to get him to take his first breath.

Watching in wide-eyed wonder, the five-year-old shouted, "Hit him again! He shouldn't have crawled up there in the first place!"

Little kids' instructions on life:

- *When your dad is mad and asks, "Do I look stupid?" don't answer him.*
- *Never try to baptize a cat.*
- *Never trust a dog to guard your hamburger.*
- *Never tell your little brother you're not going to do what your mom told you to do.*

Unless you change and become like little children, you will never enter the kingdom of heaven. (MATTHEW 18:3)

"I've reached the age where I need three pairs of glasses:
One for driving, one for reading—and one to find the other two!"

August 19

Finally the beggar died and was carried by the angels to be with Abraham in the place of the righteous dead.
(LUKE 16:22 TLB)

A farmer was taking his little boy to a distant place. While walking they came to a rickety bridge over a turbulent stream. The little boy was afraid, so the father said, "Son, I'll hold your hand." With careful steps they crossed the bridge together. That was in the daylight.

The night shadows were falling when they returned. The lad said, "Father, what about that stream? And that rickety old bridge? I'm frightened."

The big, powerful farmer reached down, took the little fellow in his arms, and said, "Now you'll feel safe." As the farmer neared the turbulent stream, the boy fell asleep in his father's arms. The next morning the boy woke up, safe at home. The sun was streaming through the window. He never even knew when he crossed the dangerous bridge over the turbulent waters.

That is the death of a Christian.

It is a great comfort to know that God has His hands on the steering wheel of the universe.

And I saw the dead, great and small, standing before the throne. Then books were opened, and the book of life was opened. The dead were judged by what they had done, which was written in the books. (REVELATION 20:12 NCV)

God's love can happen anywhere. Once it happened to me at the Department of Motor Vehicles office when I was selecting a personalized license plate for Bill. As I looked through the giant book of license-plate names that had already been used, I realized that my own name is written in another book that is much more important—the Lamb's Book of Life—and that I am forever a daughter of the King. I am royalty! At that moment, God's warm comfort blanket enfolded me with the assurance of His care. I felt His presence so strongly that I had tears in my eyes. The warm comforting feeling of His love splashed over me—even at the DMV!

Love is the only disease that makes you feel better.

August 21

The steadfast love of the LORD never ceases, his mercies never come to an end; they are new every morning; great is your faithfulness. (LAMENTATIONS 3:22–23 NRSV)

When our boys were young, we trained them to always check the refrigerator door for notes from us. Typing has always been faster than handwriting for me, so I would type the list of chores I expected of each of them. Even though I tried to divide the work evenly, one day Larry complained that he had too much stuff on his list. "I'll *never* get all this done!" he pouted.

When we compared all the boys' notes, the problem quickly became apparent. Barney, who was then ten, had redone all the notes, laboriously retyping them (with one finger) and redistributing all of HIS chores to the other three brothers! Then he signed the notes "MOM" and even put on some of my lipstick and blotted his lips to imprint a "kiss," just as I always did!

No matter how smart we are, weary mothers need lots of help and encouragement—the kind that comes from family and friends, and especially the kind that comes from God.

Anxious hearts are very heavy but a word of encouragement does wonders! (PROVERBS 12:25 TLB)

It's easy to be an encourager. We can encourage someone with a cheery phone call, a quick visit— or just a smile. One of my favorite ways to encourage others is by writing a quick note. Usually I jot something down on a silly cartoon I've seen somewhere. It doesn't have to be long. Brief and sincere notes can uplift the receivers much as a bouquet of flowers—perhaps more. If you find it hard to express yourself, begin by telling your friend about some kindness she has done for you. Remind her how much her friendship means to you, then offer your own encouragement to her.

So many hearts need to be filled up with hope. As I speak around the country, I look out over the audiences and imagine hearts that are squashed down, stamped on, flattened out from thoughtless deeds done to them, or shriveled and dying from lack of encouragement. What happiness it brings ME to share a glad word with those hurting hearts and restore them with an infusion of God's hope!

We're not put on this earth to see through each other, but to see each other through.

August 23

Come to Me, all you who labor and are heavy laden, and I will give you rest. (MATTHEW 11:28 NKJV)

It may be hard to see how you can let go and give your loved one to God. One way is to picture in your mind that you are putting him or her into a gift box. Then, in your mind's eye, wrap the box with lovely paper and ribbon. Next, picture a long flight of stairs. At the top is the throne of God, with Jesus sitting on it. Imagine yourself climbing up those stairs, carrying your beautifully wrapped package. When you get to the top, put the box at Jesus' feet. Watch Him bend down to pick up the package and place it on His lap. Picture Jesus opening your package and tenderly taking your loved one into His arms.

You must be sure that Jesus has your loved one in His grip, and you must believe that He will *never* let go. You have given your loved one to Jesus. He will take over.

Do not ask the Lord for a life free from grief; instead ask for courage that endures.

*Take My yoke upon you and learn from Me, for I am
gentle and lowly in heart, and you will find rest for your
souls. For My yoke is easy and My burden is light.*
(MATTHEW 11:29–30 NKJV)

Now comes the crucial moment. Turn around.
Then walk back down the stairs. Halfway down,
pause and see that your loved one is safe in Jesus'
arms. Hear Jesus saying, "No one will ever take this
precious one out of My hands." As you
continue walking down the stairs, thank
God for taking control. Then, pray,
*Lord, that settles it. I have given (name)
to You and have taken my hands off.*

Copy this simple drawing
and post it someplace
to continually remind
you that you have
given your loved
one to God.

It is more blessed to give than to receive. (ACTS 20:35)

It's healthy to laugh at yourself. A friend sent me a pair of bunny slippers, and every now and then I put them on, especially when I'm tempted to start feeling self-important or a little blue. There's something about bunny slippers that keeps my perspective where it belongs. But in addition to that, my bunny slippers remind me that whatever happens, I can still be a little silly and laugh and enjoy life. Pain dissolves, frustrations vanish, and burdens roll away when I have on my bunny slippers.

Silly slippers make a great gift for someone who's hospitalized. As I was leaving the hospital recently after visiting a friend, I passed a patient slowly walking the hall wearing ridiculous house shoes shaped like terrified chickens. "My friend gave them to me," she explained with a smile as I stared at her feet. "She calls them my antidepression shoes. And I have to admit, everywhere I wear them, people laugh. And that makes me laugh. So if I want to be depressed, I have to take them off!"

Live each day as if it were your last. Someday you'll be right.

When you talk, do not say harmful things, but say what people need—words that will help others become stronger.
(EPHESIANS 4:29 NCV)

R ecently, my good friend Lynda and I were driving to Yucaipa, California, for a weekend conference at a Baptist church where I was to be the featured speaker. I had gotten up feeling a little weary that morning, and as we drove, I whined, "I'm so tired of spreading my joy. I just wish I could stay home and never have to tell my story again." I was ticking off all my symptoms of burnout when we rounded a curve and a huge highway billboard loomed up ahead of us. In letters that seemed twenty feet high, it said:

SPREAD YOUR JOY!

In smaller letters near the bottom, the sign said, "Paid for by First Baptist Church, Yucaipa"—the very place we were headed! Talk about SOMEONE sending me a message! We were still laughing when we got to the church, where we had one of the best conferences ever. Afterward, I realized again that in spreading my joy, God had restored ME.

LAUGHTER is contagious . . . Start an epidemic!

August 27

Charm is deceptive, and beauty is fleeting; but a woman who fears the LORD is to be praised. (PROVERBS 31:30)

After leading twelve thousand women at a Women of Faith conference in a rousing chorus of "I'll Fly Away," this anonymous note was left at my book table:

> Just wanted to tell you how big of a smile was on my face as we sang "I'll Fly Away." . . . My mom . . . told us the story of my grandmother singing "I'll Fly Away" at the top of her lungs. When she got to the chorus, she had forgotten the words, but that didn't stop her. She just improvised and kept right on singing. When she got to "When I die . . ." she sang, "When I *do,* hallelujah, *doo-dee-doo,* I'll fly away." My sisters and I will sing it that way 'til the day we "do." (I mean "die.")

I'll never hear that song again without thinking of that spunky grandmother belting out her homemade lyrics with great joy and gusto!

May your joys be added, your sorrows subtracted, your friends multiplied, and your enemies divided.

The gate is small and the road is narrow that leads to true life. (MATTHEW 7:14 NCV)

This verse reminds us how easily we can stumble off the narrow road to heaven. But it also reminds us there's a drop-off area outside the gate where we lay down our earthly treasures: the bank deposits, jewelry, homes, and cars. All our worries must be dropped there, too, along with broken hearts and tears.

My daughter-in-love, Shannon, has beautifully described how one of her and Barney's friends "gradually let go of the things of the world and grasped the things of heaven" as he neared the end of a ten-year struggle with cancer. During his remarkable transition he gradually released the initial anxiety he'd felt when first diagnosed and the frustration that had tormented him and gently reached for the peace that seemed to flow out of heaven and wrap him in God's comfort blanket. When he died, the friend understood that he was taking nothing with him, Shannon said, "except the love of those whose lives he had touched."

In the end, we release our desperate grip on the lifeline . . . and fall into the arms of everlasting life.

August 29

A time to get, and a time to lose; a time to keep, and a time to cast away. (ECCLESIASTES 3:6 KJV)

When a man was moving to a new town, his friends bought him a young sapling to plant in his new home as a reminder of all the fun they had shared. The man nurtured the tree, and soon it was taller than he was. Each spring its blossoms lifted his spirits and reminded him of his friends. But then he had to move again. He called a tree expert and insisted, "No matter what the expense, I want to take it with me."

But the specialist shook his head. "This tree won't live where you're going," he said. "The climate's too harsh. All you can do is tell the new owners its story and help them understand how special it is."

That's how many of us ended up with the Tree of Life taking root in our hearts. Its seed was a gift from someone else who had nurtured it in his own life—and then passed it on to us. What an awesome hand-me-down!

Jesus' gift to us is something we don't deserve, didn't work for, and can't buy for any price.

Uphold my steps in Your paths, / That my footsteps may not slip. (Psalm 17:5 NKJV)

In my years of working in Spatula Ministries, I've been asked just about every kind of question by parents of gay children. Often their confused and be-fuddled letters show that they're writing while trying to cope with the initial shock of learning that their child is gay. Been there, done that! My mail has included one letter that began "Dear Spatula MISERIES" and this one, which confused a "leper" with a zoo animal:

> My son is a homosexual. He keeps asking why we are treating him like a leopard. What does he mean? What does he think we are doing . . . operating a zoo?

One lady confused her daughter's problem with a celebrity's nationality—Lebanese. She wrote, "My daughter . . . talks about being a lesbian. Isn't that what Danny Thomas is? What does that have to do with girls writing love letters to each other?"

Dear Barbara, I've practiced enough for the Rapture. Would you please call God on your hot line and tell Him we're ready?

Brothers and sisters, do not complain against each other or you will be judged guilty. (JAMES 5:9 NCV)

Letters of inquiry and complaint sent to newspaper consumer-assistance Action columns:

- "Three months after buying a couch, the place where I sit developed an indentation."

- "I bought a recliner. It has a flaw on the *toot* rest."

- "Is it possible when I die to have the body legally declared dead?"

- "The directions on my hair conditioner say to squeeze excess water from hair and shake well before using, but it gives me a headache to shake my head that hard."

- "Do any of the mortuaries around here have cremation? If so, can you manage to get it before you die to make sure you have it?"

- "Once a week I bowl with the girls. Do I burn up enough calories to eat a sundae afterward?"

It doesn't take a dictionary to learn the language of love.

I have scattered them among the nations, but in those faraway places, they will remember me. They and their children will live and return. (ZECHARIAH 10:9 NCV)

Happy first of September! As school begins, summer winds down, and the first hints of gold appear on the trees. This is a time of year when families look ahead with anticipation to the new school year and all the excitement it brings while remembering the summer fun they shared as the trees were sending forth their buds, blossoms, and then their lush, green foliage. And once we've started that nostalgic look back, it's hard to stop! With the kids at school, we glance out the window and see reminders of earlier times, even earlier years, when the swing set was crawling with kids, the bicycle was spinning down the driveway, or the soccer ball was being kicked around the backyard.

Memories of times spent together are precious. Make sure you fill them with love and trim them with laughter. And on a September day many years from now, you'll be glad you did!

The heart is like a treasure chest that's filled with souvenirs; it's where we keep the memories we've gathered through the years.

September 2

I ask only one thing from the LORD. This is what I want: Let me live in the LORD's house all my life. (PSALM 27:4 NCV)

Some homes seem to have laughter built into their walls. It seems to be magically absorbed into the structure from the laughter of the people living inside. Get some fun in your life today, and when your house is empty, you'll be comforted by the laughter that's exuded from those walls.

I was reminded of this idea when I read about a church youth group in Iowa that bought three hundred two-by-fours for a local Habitat for Humanity project. Before the material was used in framing the house, on each board the thoughtful Christians wrote messages of love and joy to the future homeowners.

Knowing that the framework of your home is inscribed with Scripture verses and messages of love—and with laughter—how could you be anything but joyful each time you entered? That's surely how our mansions in heaven will feel as we step through the doors into a place infused with God's love.

An optimist builds castles in the air. A dreamer lives there. A realist collects the rent from both of them.

Do not reject me when I am old; do not leave me when my strength is gone. (PSALM 71:9 NCV)

My class reunion's coming,
    and I don't know what to do.
My weight and chins have doubled
    since the year of '42.
I look into the mirror and—Good grief!
    How can this be?
Gray hair, false teeth, thick glasses—
    It's my mother's face I see!

But I head out to the party.
    No sense moping, I decide.
I'll just have to grin and bear it.
    (But I'm dying, deep inside.)
Then I walk into the banquet hall and stop.
    There's some mistake.
Not a single classmate do I find.
    Did I confuse the date?
Still, the faces seem familiar,
    as each one I keenly stare at . . .
Then I realize I'm looking at—Good grief!
    My classmates' parents!
        —ANN LUNA

Nostalgia isn't what it used to be.

September 4

I will always have hope and will praise you more and more. (PSALM 71:14 NCV)

Encouragement can mean a lot, even to those accustomed to receiving it. Mark Twain confessed that he could "live for three weeks on a single compliment." Chuck Swindoll describes encouragement as a "hope transplant" to someone in need. The late Erma Bombeck, a talented encourager, wrote in her last column, published just five days before she died:

> My deeds will be measured not by my youthful appearance, but by the concern lines on my forehead, the laugh lines around my mouth, and the chins from seeing what can be done for those smaller than me or who have fallen.

I hope *my* spirit is wrinkled and lined from being pressed against God. As Hudson Taylor said, "It doesn't matter how great the pressure is. What really matters is *where the pressure lies,* whether it comes between me and God or whether it presses me nearer His heart." Romans 8:39 says, NOTHING can separate us from the love of God. He *wallpapers* our hearts to His.

The eternal stars shine out as soon as it is dark enough.

Surely goodness and mercy shall follow me All the days of my life; / And I will dwell in the house of the LORD / Forever. (PSALM 23:6 NKJV)

During a conference in a remote area, I stayed in a cabin nestled below a train trestle. All night, I heard the trains passing. The next morning at breakfast several of the women complained about the trains that had disrupted their sleep during the night. "Didn't they bother you, Barbara?" one of them asked.

Actually I had rather enjoyed it. Hearing the passing trains, I reminisced about the times when I was a child visiting my aunt, who lived where trains were heard in the night. What warmth that memory brought. That night I listened to the first faraway toots of each train's whistle as it came to a crossing. Then I pictured it approaching, passing by, and speeding on through the night.

These days the only train whistle I can hear is the steam locomotive at Knott's Berry Farm. How fortunate I felt that night to hear those clacking sounds as the trains rumbled across the trestle above my head and sped off into the night.

What a gift it is to find joy in the small things.

September 6

Store up for yourselves treasures in heaven, where moth and rust do not destroy, and where thieves do not break in and steal. (MATTHEW 6:20)

In an insightful essay, writer J. Anne Drummond pointed out that "one day all the keepsakes we store in the backs of our closets will be taken by our loved ones to save in *their* closets or sold to someone else or thrown away. But the treasures of love and personal friendship with Jesus Christ can never be taken from us."

In my childhood home, a plaque hung on the wall to remind all of us, "Only one life, 'twill soon be past. Only what's done for Christ will last." Somehow those lines still help me today to get a better perspective on my life here on earth and remember that what we do in this short life counts toward ETERNITY! We can't take anything WITH us, but we can send love on ahead—by sharing Christ's love with those who are in need here.

The average person probably hasn't stored up enough treasure in heaven to even make a down payment for a harp!

For where your treasure is, there your heart will be also.
(MATTHEW 6:21)

This sign outside an empty,
flood-stricken house offered a lesson in faith.

**Life is 10 percent what happens to you and 90 percent
how you respond to it.** —CHARLES SWINDOLL

September 8

Isaac . . . said, "Ah, the smell of my son is like the smell of a field that the LORD has blessed." (GENESIS 27:27)

Smells trigger our memories today, just as they did for Isaac hundreds of years ago. Smell our wood smoke somewhere, and you may recall a campfire gathering or be transported back in time to a late-autumn day when smoke rose from fireplace chimneys or woodstoves in your neighborhood. The scent of rubbing alcohol makes us remember childhood shots. For me, the sweet, old-fashioned perfume of purple lilacs evokes the ghosts of childhood backyards with brick walls and dense shade trees. And the smell of damp wool will always make me think of wet mittens with icy cuffs, snowballs, and apple-cheeked kids coming in out of the sub-zero cold in my childhood home in Michigan.

Our ears and noses can teach us as much about life as any book. Be alert to the smells in the air that can trigger your memories and make you feel alive.

Albert Einstein said, "There are two ways to live your life. One is as though nothing is a miracle. The other is as though everything is a miracle."

Be strong and take heart, all you who hope in the LORD.
(PSALM 31:24)

The cutest illustration of hope I've found is about a little boy who stood at the foot of the escalator in a big department store, intently watching the handrail. He never took his eyes off the handrail as the escalator rolled upward in front of him. A salesperson finally asked him if he was lost. The little fellow replied, "Nope. I'm just waiting for my chewing gum to come back."

If your face is in the dust, if you are in a wringer situation, be like the little boy waiting for his chewing gum to come back. Stand firm, be patient, and trust God. Then get busy with your life . . . there is work to do.

She that lives in hope dances without a fiddle.

September 10

Do not lose heart. Though outwardly we are wasting away, yet inwardly we are being renewed day by day. (2 CORINTHIANS 4:16)

A mother sent me this note:

Dear Barb (and Gopher Bill),

Like the sundial, this year I am only going to count the sunny hours! I don't know where we are—I don't need to know. I just know it's all in His hands. How much safer could it be?

This dear lady's words remind me that nothing touches me that has not passed through the hands of my heavenly Father—NOTHING! Whatever occurs, God has sovereignly surveyed and approved it. We may never know why, but we do know our pain is no accident to Him who guides our lives. He is in no way surprised by any of it. Before it ever touches us, it passes through Him.

People are like tea bags. You have to put them in hot water before you know how strong they are.

Children, obey your parents in the Lord, for this is right.
(EPHESIANS 6:1 NKJV)

THE FAMILY CIRCUS®　　　**By Bil Keane**

"I'm grounded. I said one more word
to my mother."

*School days are the happiest days of your life—providing,
of course, your kids are old enough to go.* —PAUL SELDEN

September 12

Great is our Lord and mighty in power; his understanding has no limit. (PSALM 147:5)

The wife of a pastor who had served his denomination for well over twenty-five years wrote an anonymous article in her denominational paper, telling of the shock she and her husband felt when they learned their son was gay. During one of their talks with their son, the mother asked him if he knew how much he had hurt them. His answer cut deep into her heart: "Do you know how much I've hurt all these years? I didn't choose to be this way!"

In response, these parents devoted themselves to unconditionally loving their son. In her article, the mother wrote, "The homosexually oriented person needs more of the very thing we too often go out of our way to deny them. We must love as Jesus loves—unconditionally." She noted that without the tremendous support of other parents of gays "who were willing to share their own journey, we would have died." She and her husband said they had found only one thing they could do to help their homosexual son, and they had made that one thing their motto.

From this moment on . . . LOVE!

I am quiet now before the Lord, just as a child who is weaned from the breast. Yes, my begging has been stilled. O Israel, you too should quietly trust in the Lord—now, and always. (PSALM 131:2–3 TLB)

My child...

Trust me.

I have everything under control.

Jesus

September 14

Blessed are the people who know the joyful sound!
(Psalm 89:15 NKJV)

As I waited in a little room before my routine medical exam, I couldn't help but overhear my doctor speaking on the phone in the next room. He was saying, "Oh, you'll be fine . . . you'll be just fine!" A little later, I heard voices outside in the hallway, along with the sound of tapping, made by an older person with a cane, perhaps. Then I heard the doctor say, "Why, yes, Joe, you'll be fine . . . you'll be just fine!"

In a few minutes, the doctor came in and asked me cheerfully, "Well, how are you doing today?" My response was, "Well, it doesn't really matter because I know I will be FINE, JUST FINE!" We laughed as I confessed to my unintentional eavesdropping. He examined me, and we chatted a moment more. Then as I was leaving, he added, "You're going to be fine—just fine!"

Walking to the car, I was thankful for my doctor's positive attitude. Instead of some gloomy prognosis, I much prefer to hear, "You'll be FINE, JUST FINE!"

I'm too blest to be stressed!

The gift of God is eternal life in Christ Jesus our Lord.
(ROMANS 6:23 NKJV)

When Bill and I were meeting recently with our insurance agent, he consulted some actuarial tables and told me my life expectancy was another nineteen years. The poor man probably expected me to be a little sad to hear this prediction. I was sad, all right, but not in the way he expected. As he delivered this bit of news, my face automatically wrinkled up into a frown, and I spouted off, "Ugh! I don't wanna wait *that* long!"

It's not that I'm living a miserable life. On the contrary, I've made it a habit to wring out of every single day all the fun and love I can find. Sometimes it seems I have the best of both worlds—overflowing joy here and the promise of eternal happiness in paradise. Still, I know that my pleasantest day here on earth is *nothing* compared with the unfathomable joy that awaits me in heaven.

I'm a child of the King . . . living in palace preparation mode.

With God nothing is impossible. (LUKE 1:37 NKJV)

A story recounted by Reeve Lindbergh, Charles Lindbergh's daughter, illustrates how easy it is to be consumed with insignificant details while ignoring something wonderful. In 1997, Reeve was invited to speak at the Smithsonian Institution's commemoration of her father's historic solo flight across the Atlantic. Museum officials invited her to arrive before the facility opened that day so she could have a closeup look at the little plane, suspended from the museum ceiling, that her father had piloted from New York to Paris in 1927. Reeve and her young son, Ben, eagerly climbed into the bucket of a cherry-picker that carried them upward. Seeing the machine that her father had so bravely flown across the sea was an un-forgettable experience for Reeve. She tenderly touched the door handle, knowing her father must have grasped it many times with his own hand. With tears in her eyes, she whispered, "Oh, Ben, isn't this amazing?"

"Yeaaaaah," Ben replied, equally impressed. "I've never been in a cherry-picker before!"

If God is your copilot . . . swap seats!

Don't keep on scolding and nagging your children, making them angry and resentful. Rather, bring them up with the loving discipline the Lord himself approves, with suggestions and godly advice. (EPHESIANS 6:4 TLB)

More truths brought to us by children:

- Don't let your mom brush your hair when she's mad at your dad.

- If your sister hits you, don't hit her back. It's always the second person who gets caught.

- Dogs still have bad breath even after a squirt of breath freshener.

- Never hold the cat while the vacuum cleaner is running.

- When you're in trouble the best place to be is in Grandma's lap.

With enough practice, joy becomes as natural as breathing, and such a habit that it just comes out of your body.

—LINDA DAVENPORT, *KANSAS CITY STAR*

September 18

If we live in the light, as God is in the light, we can share fellowship with each other. (1 JOHN 1:7 NCV)

When I spoke at the Los Angeles Rescue Mission, Bill came along and sat on the platform behind me—which turned out not to be such a good idea. Because he had a bad cold, he kept nipping at a little bottle of cough medicine. Of course, it looked as if he were nipping at something else!

As I began my talk, one of the mission workers came down the aisle carrying a pole, almost twenty feet long with some kind of gripping device on the end. He stopped at the front row and swung the pole toward a man who had his hat pulled down around his ears. In one quick motion he snatched the man's hat right off his head, then turned and walked out. Nobody seemed to notice—except me, and I was so flabbergasted, I burst out laughing! The mission rules prohibited wearing hats in the audience, but apparently there were no rules about throwing speakers for a loop by plucking off hats with a twenty-foot pole.

Bumper Snicker: *Blessings Happen!*

*In the sweat of your face you shall eat bread / Till you
return to the ground, / For out of it you were taken; /
For dust you are, / And to dust you shall return.*
(GENESIS 3:19 NKJV)

A tale from the village of Confusion Corners:

Lola and Ned sat at the same bingo table and often
walked home together. They took the shortcut
through the adjacent cemetery.

One night Ned left early, so Lola had to walk
home alone. Halfway through the cemetery she
heard a faint noise—a voice calling, "Help, help."
As Lola approached an open grave site, the voice
was stronger. She peered down into the grave, and
there lay Ned.

"Help me," he said. "I'm freezing."

Lola had a puzzled look on her face as she said to
herself, *Ned is dead? I must have forgotten.* She said,
"Of course I'll help you, Ned. You stay quiet while I
get someone. No wonder you're cold. You've kicked
off all your dirt."

When did my wild oats turn into shredded wheat?

September 20

I will make rivers flow on barren heights, and springs within the valleys. I will turn the desert into pools of water, and the parched ground into springs.
(ISAIAH 41:18)

A gardener irrigating his garden was able to channel life-giving water to all areas except for one little dying plant way over in the corner. The gardener knew if he had just one more piece of irrigation pipe he could get water to that wilting plant and transform it with new life. So it is with the Master Gardener. Because He chooses to minister through us, He needs many lengths of pipe to bless persons here, there, and all around. Perhaps in your area there is a drooping, wilting person who needs God's touch right now. We can be that extra piece of pipe—a conduit through which He channels His cheer, encouragement, and joy to those in need.

May your day be fashioned with joy, sprinkled with dreams, and touched by the miracle of love.

The autumn rains fill [the valley] with pools of water. The people get stronger as they go, and everyone meets with God in Jerusalem. (PSALM 84:6–7 NCV)

Today's the first day of autumn, the perfect time to gather your loved ones around you and tell them they're loved. Watch them get stronger as your words sink in!

> Do you want to say you love me?
> Say it now, while I can hear
> Your voice, soft, low, and soothing,
> gently telling me I'm dear.
> Do you want to show you love me?
> Hold my hand, caress my cheek,
> And then just listen—only listen—to my
> thoughts and hurts and dreams.
> Age will change us, time will turn us,
> death will take us all too soon.
> Do you want to say you love me?
> Say it now. I'll say it too.
> —ANN LUNA

The best and most beautiful things in the world cannot be seen, or even touched, they must be felt with the heart.
—HELEN KELLER

September 22

Out of the abundance of the heart the mouth speaks.
(MATTHEW 12:34 NKJV)

It would be wonderful if husbands and dads could open up and drain off some of their pent-up feelings when a son or daughter dies or when an adult child announces that he or she is homosexual. But the truth is, in most cases *that's not going to happen!* Women talk and talk, and as the hurt drains out, their pain is dissipated. Men, on the other hand, hear bad news once, and they don't want to hear it again. They don't want to talk about it; they want to go play golf or fish and FORGET about it. And they can't do that if you keep bringing it up (which is what YOU need to do!). We expect men to be strong and supportive in crises. But grief is the one area they cannot deal with. So I advise women to find another Christian WOMAN to pour out their hearts to. Find a sister or a trusted friend who will spend some time with you and listen non-judgmentally.

Sympathy is YOUR pain in MY heart.

It takes wisdom to have a good family, and it takes understanding to make it strong. (PROVERBS 24:3 NCV)

© 1990 John McPherson. Used by permission of John McPherson.
Included in *McPherson's Marriage Album* (Grand Rapids: Zondervan, 1991).

There are two times when a man doesn't understand a woman—before marriage and after marriage.

September 24

The LORD is close to the brokenhearted, and he saves those whose spirits have been crushed. (PSALM 34:18 NCV)

When a Spatula friend noticed that the anniversary of Tim's death was coming up, she shared an idea from a bereaved father in a Compassionate Friends group:

> Everyone important had a holiday, he said. Well, the most important person to him was his Kathy. . . . So he chose the day of her death as Kathy's holiday. He would take the day off work if it wasn't a weekend, and each year he'd first go to the cemetery, telling Kathy about the happenings in the family. Then he'd spend the rest of the day doing something he knew she'd approve of, like visiting a museum, taking a day trip, a drive to the beach, whatever.
>
> All of us who have lost a special treasure and hear of this idea think it's pretty neat. . . . And it's much easier to have that day approaching and thinking of it as a tribute day to our person than a day for just dreaded and frightful memories!

The secret to joyful living is celebrating SOMETHING every day, no matter how insignificant it may be.

He will . . . fill your mouth with laughter and your lips with shouts of joy. (JOB 8:21)

I t's the way we live our lives—our attitudes and our actions—that determines what stage of life we're in. You may have a husband in the throes of a midlife crisis, parents who are struggling to remember what decade they're in, and adult children who are giving you fits, but if you can keep breathing and laughing, you'll survive (at least until it's your turn to move into the Home for the Bewildered and try to remember what decade it is!).

Anyone can laugh—whether you're mobile or bedridden, active or lame, whether you're equipped with single or double eyes, arms, ears, legs, and kidneys! No physical limitation can prevent you from laughing. Even if some problem has robbed you of your voice, you can still laugh with your eyes. And if for some reason your eyes can't sparkle anymore, you can still smile in your heart.

Remember: The more you complain, the longer God lets you live. *"Delight yourself in the LORD and he will give you the desires of your heart."* **(PSALM 37:4)**

September 26

Heaven and earth will pass away, but My words will by no means pass away. (MATTHEW 24:35 NKJV)

Someone told me about an elegant fashion show organized several years ago by a church women's group. The guests were rewarded with several door prizes, and one frail but spirited ninety-year-old lady burst into laughter as she opened the gift she'd won— a *twenty-year* goal-planner. Shaking her head and laughing happily, she quickly handed it to a much younger woman at her table. "Honey, I hope to heaven I won't be needing this!" she said with a merry twinkle in her eye.

That woman didn't need a place to write down her goals for the next twenty years; at that point her main goal was arriving at heaven's gates and moving into her mansion—and her new, perpetually youthful body!

Benefits of growing older: *In a hostage situation, you are likely to be released first.*

You who are his angels, praise the LORD.
(PSALM 103:20 NCV)

We should always be aware of opportunities to do the work of angels. That was the case when a kindhearted woman spotted a little boy standing bare-footed in front of a New York City shoe store one cold November day. "What are you looking at?" she asked.

"I was asking God to give me a pair of those shoes," the little boy replied.

The woman took the little boy inside the store, asked a clerk to bring her a warm, wet towel, then knelt in front of the boy and gently wiped his feet. Next she took several pairs of socks off the rack, asked the clerk to bring the shoes he'd been eyeing in the window, put the socks on his feet, and laced up the shoes to make sure they fit.

"You'll be more comfortable now," she told the boy, smiling, as she paid the bill.

The astonished lad looked up in her face. "Are you God's wife?" he asked.

We are each of us angels with only one wing. And we can only fly by embracing each other. —LUCIANO DE CRESCENZO

September 28

A friend loves you all the time. (PROVERBS 17:17 NCV)

Make a friendship kit:

Rubber bands: To hold friends close

Tissues: To dry a tear

Recipes: To make and share

Stationery: To write notes of encouragement

Band-Aids: Reminders that friends help heal
a hurting heart

Poems: To express your love

Prayers: To lead your friend to God

* * *

Put your arms around each other
(This page 1 banner headline appeared in The Tennessean
*on April 18, 1998, quoting Mayor Phil Bredesen the day
after a devastating tornado ravaged much of East Nashville.)*

The teachings of the LORD are perfect; they give new strength. The rules of the LORD can be trusted; they make plain people wise. (PSALM 19:7 NCV)

We live in an imperfect world with people who are full of quirks and in homes that have imperfections. I have a friend who saved and scrimped to buy some expensive wallpaper for her son's bedroom. It finally arrived after being special-ordered, and she brought it home and put it away, planning to hang it as soon as she found the time.

Her husband discovered the wallpaper one day while she was out shopping and decided to surprise her by hanging it himself. So he worked all day, papering the entire bedroom with the lovely new paper. He made only one mistake: He hung all the paper UPSIDE DOWN. It was supposed to show colorful balloons with strings hanging down. Instead all the strings climbed up the wall like slithering snakes.

When my friend returned, she was shocked, but there was nothing to be done. Learning to live with upside-down situations isn't easy, but it is part of life.

Nothing is foolproof to a sufficiently talented fool.

September 30

Woe to those who are wise in their own eyes, / And prudent in their own sight! (ISAIAH 5:21 NKJV)

IF WOMEN CONTROLLED MEDICINE

But one thing I do: Forgetting what is behind and straining toward what is ahead, I press on toward the goal. (PHILIPPIANS 3:13–14)

Because I've said so many times that I celebrate the first of the month, I sometimes have to postpone my celebrations because I'm so busy telling callers how I'm celebrating! Sometimes East Coast friends call me at 5 A.M. California time to ask how I'm going to celebrate. Sometimes it's noon before I even have time to brush my teeth because of all the well-wishers calling to celebrate "our" day with me.

Maybe I just send a funny card that I'm sure will brighten someone's day. Or I try a different hairstyle or buy a new pair of earrings. Or I change the sheets and hang them outside to dry. There is nothing as fragrant and fun as fresh, clean sheets dried outdoors! Recently I parked on a high bluff overlooking a freeway and just sat there watching and listening to a new Gaither tape. This is MY DAY to pamper myself, a time to replenish and renew. After all . . .

You can't give anything away if your own tank is empty.

October 2

We found trouble all around us. We had fighting on the outside and fear on the inside. But God, who comforts those who are troubled, comforted us.
(2 CORINTHIANS 7:5–6 NCV)

About three months after Steve died in Vietnam, his duffel bag arrived at our door. In his wallet, stained and torn, was my last letter to him. It had arrived the very morning of the ambush in which Steve had been killed. My letter said, in part:

> Whether you are at home . . . or over there in Vietnam, you are still SAFE in God's hands, and even if your life would be sacrificed for us in Vietnam, even THEN, Steve, you are safe in the arms of Jesus. . . . Even death, should it come to us, . . . brings us just a step closer to God and to eternity, because we have placed our faith in Jesus Christ.

I had kissed my signature, and now the lipstick was smeared, but that didn't matter. The letter was a symbol of the hope Steve had in Christ and of the family back home who loved him and shared that hope with him.

Mothers hold their children's hands for a while . . . their hearts forever.

God will have a house for us. It will not be a house made by human hands; instead, it will be a home in heaven that will last forever. (2 CORINTHIANS 5:1 NCV)

If you grew up in a loving family, you're probably familiar with that strong, nurturing sense of welcome that wraps around you the instant you step inside the door. It's an atmosphere, a feeling that engulfs you like a soft, warm cloud. It's the sound of footsteps rushing toward you, the tinkle of laughter bubbling up from someone who's glad to see you. It's the light in a window and the spark in a loved one's eyes. In short, it's *home.*

That's surely the feeling, multiplied ten thousand times, we'll have as we fly through the clouds and find ourselves in heaven. What joy we'll experience! What a welcome we'll receive! What love we'll know! All these glorious feelings will flood over us, and we'll be spellbound with wonder. Best of all, we'll finally hear the Master say those precious words we've longed for through all of earth's trials: *"Welcome HOME!"*

Bumper sticker (punctuated with a bold cross): *No matter which direction I'm heading, I'm homeward bound!*

October 4

 friend sent me this darling idea . . . and I can't wait to see if she's right!

"Barb, we'll know how to find you in heaven. Your mansion will have geraniums all around it!"

Whatever is good and perfect comes to us from God, the Creator of all light, and he shines forever without change or shadow. (JAMES 1:17 TLB)

We have a clock in our car that is always one hour off from October to April when the time changes. The mechanism that changes the dial is broken, and during those months I have to keep remembering that the clock is one hour ahead of life. Having to keep adjusting my time and schedule according to a clock that is one hour off may be teaching me something. Some things in life are *never* what they should be, and we have to adjust. Being willing to adjust to something less than perfect is a sign of acceptance.

Life is never perfect, but Jesus is. And He takes the imperfections—the broken pieces and the messes—and turns them into hope. Remember, no matter what trial you're going through, it didn't come to stay. It came to pass. You may be living in a set of parentheses, but whatever you're going through won't last forever.

Only some of us learn from other people's mistakes; the rest of us have to be the other people.

October 6

Love is as strong as death. . . . Love bursts into flames and burns like a hot fire. (SONG OF SOLOMON 8:6 NCV)

Although I love fireplaces, we don't have one in our home. I've often missed it—until recently. To add to my Joy Room collection, someone sent me a twenty-minute video of a roaring fire, complete with the crackling, popping sounds that only a fire can make. So now I just sit back in a nice easy chair and for twenty minutes I watch a roaring fire start up, burn merrily, and then diminish into glowing embers. I can almost smell the wood burning!

When people ask me, "How do you unwind after a busy day?" I tell them I enjoy a long bubble bath and then I "play my fireplace"!

It's not always easy being a joyful woman. Most of us are more experienced in grumbling than glowing. But to those who've learned to "count it all joy," the boomerang blessings far outnumber the bruises.

For I was hungry and you fed me; . . . naked and you clothed me. (MATTHEW 25:35–36 TLB)

Dear Esther," the letter said, "I'll be passing through the area Saturday and would like to visit. Love always, Jesus."

Saturday? Why, that's today! Esther's hands shook with excitement as she checked her pocketbook—nothing but a five-dollar bill. She rushed out to buy sandwich fixings. As she came out of the store, a homeless couple stopped her. "Lady, could you help us?"

"I'd like to, but I'm in a hurry," she called over her shoulder. Then she turned around. "Here, take this sandwich stuff. I've got a can of soup at home I can serve my guest." Then she noticed the woman was shivering in the cold. "I've got another jacket at home," she said, pulling her arms out of the sleeves. "You take this one."

"Thank you, lady!" the poor couple called as the woman hurried on. When she got home a note was stuck in her door. "Dear Esther," it said. "So good to see you again. Thanks for the delicious sandwiches. And the coat is beautiful. Love always, Jesus."

Church sign: *Give God what's right. Not what's left.*

October 8

The fruit of the Spirit is love, joy, peace, patience, kindness, goodness, faithfulness, gentleness and self-control. (GALATIANS 5:22–23)

Bill and I were driving through Palm Springs, the famous desert resort community, when we came upon a roadside stand advertising "Desert Sweetened Grapefruit." I thought, *That's the way it is with all of us when we go through a desert experience—when we're out there in the barren and dry wastes, not seeming to receive any encouragement from anybody. That's the time God uses to sweeten us as we learn to give our problems completely to Him.*

When we pray in Jesus' name, God has promised to listen. All we have to do is . . . do it!

Give all your worries to him, because he cares about you.
(1 PETER 5:7 NCV)

There are several steps in the process of giving a problem completely to God. You take your first step when life rises up to knock you flat—you CHURN. You feel as if your insides are full of knives, chopping you up in a grinder. Your next step is to BURN. That's right, you want to kill the one who's caused your pain, and then you want to kill yourself. You literally feel as if you're burning inside.

In your third step, you YEARN. Oh, you want so much for things to change. You yearn for the happy past, and this stage often lasts the longest of all. But then you take your next step: You LEARN. You talk with others, perhaps find a support group, and you learn that you're in a long growth process. The wonderful result is that you relieve your own pain.

And finally, you take your last step. You TURN. You turn your problem over to the Lord completely by saying, "Whatever, Lord! Whatever You bring into my life, You are strong enough to get me through it."

Sorrow looks back. Worry looks around. Faith looks up.

October 10

A man leaves his father and mother and is joined to his wife in such a way that the two become one person. (GENESIS 2:24 TLB)

In most marriages, husbands and wives eventually adapt to each other's differences, no matter how eccentric they are. One of the things I've had to adapt to is that Bill is very frugal (TIGHT is the word!). For instance, when my publisher notified us that sales of my books had reached the one million mark, Bill said we ought to celebrate. He got in the car and disappeared for a while, and I imagined him arranging a little dinner party at a fancy restaurant or even shopping for some special gift—jewelry, perhaps.

Instead he came home, smiling broadly, with *two bunches of fresh asparagus!* "I know how much you love it," he said as he dropped his gift into the kitchen sink.

*A friend who is bald says he will **never** wear a turtleneck sweater. He's afraid he'll look like a roll-on deodorant! This is the same friend who said he used to use Head & Shoulders. Now he needs Mop & Glow!*

"Yes," Adam admitted, "but it was the woman you gave me who brought me some, and I ate it." Then the Lord God asked the woman, "How could you do such a thing?" "The serpent tricked me," she replied. (GENESIS 3:12–13 TLB)

Love is blind—marriage is the eye-opener.

—PAULINE THOMASON

October 12

The sufferings we have now are nothing compared to the great glory that will be shown to us. (ROMANS 8:18 NCV)

Nothing can happen to us in this life without coming through God's filter. As someone said, paraphrasing Romans 8:18, "Heaven's delights will far outweigh earth's difficulties." Whatever we must endure here is only temporary. When God permits His children to go through the furnace experiences of our lives, He keeps His eye on the clock—and His hand on the thermostat!

Many of us are in God's waiting room—and it seems we've been here forever. But we do meet such interesting people there—wonderful people who are also learning lessons as they suffer and grow. You are not alone; thousands like you are trying to find some relief from nights of loneliness.

This life is only temporary; it's the next one that lasts forever.

But let me do one thing. . . . Let me and my friends go and cry together. (JUDGES 11:37 NCV)

Who mothers mothers? It certainly isn't the kids. THEY are the ones who get up every morning determined to prove that motherhood is definitely not for wimps!

Then who really mothers mothers? Other mothers, of course! Only a mom understands when another mom needs a break from the kid-corralling crazies or just a listening ear. At Spatula, we try to put hurting moms in touch with other hurting moms so they can find comfort, help, growth—and IMPROVEMENT. Husbands are protectors and breadwinners, but they aren't always equipped to help when you're hurting. Often it's best to find a solid Christian woman friend to listen to you ventilate and release your pent-up emotions. Then you will find that you will begin to get well. You will be comforted. It really works this way!

Just when your kids are finally fit to live with . . . they're living with someone else.

October 14

It is hard to choose between the two. I want to leave this life and be with Christ, which is much better, but you need me here in my body. (PHILIPPIANS 1:23–24 NCV)

Some of the most overstressed women these days find themselves sandwiched between the exhausting job of tending their own children while also dealing with distant parents who are ill or slipping into dementia.

My friend Sue rushed a thousand miles to her mother's side when she had emergency surgery. She slept on a little cot in her mother's hospital room for several days, struggling to care for her mother while completing her work assignments with a laptop computer and cell phone. Then her teenage son called and nonchalantly told her he'd gotten his tongue pierced and the family cat had been acting strange and now refused to come out from behind the refrigerator . . . which, by the way, had stopped working.

When we're trapped in these impossible predicaments, we don't have a lot of choices. But we *can* choose to cling to the One who holds our lives in His hand. And we can choose to laugh.

God's love shines on us and produces rainbows in our lives.

Then we were filled with laughter, and we sang happy songs. . . . The LORD has done great things for us, and we are very glad. (PSALM 126:2–3 NCV)

Here's what a little laughter can do for you:

Laughter helps you relax and unwind. Just try lifting anything heavy when you're enjoying a good belly laugh. You can't do it, because your large muscles are totally relaxed.

Laughter strengthens the immune system. Research shows that when you have a really good laugh, the body produces more immunoglobulin A, the body's warrior against upper respiratory infections.

Laughter improves your circulation by increasing the heart rate and boosting the oxygen supply to the brain.

Laughter is such a powerful "vitamin" that one hospital passes out prescriptions for laughter that warn patients of *"humoroids."* And what is the cure for humoroids? "A mild *laughsitive* each day!"

Something to laugh about: *I have found at my age that going bra-less pulls all the wrinkles out of my face.*

October 16

Abide in Me, and I in you. (JOHN 15:4 NKJV)

Fear may keep us limping in the dark, but grace keeps us walking in the light. Remember: God has not promised to give us all the answers, but He *has* promised His grace. The Lord's promise in John 15:4 enables me to say in every circumstance, "For THIS I need Jesus." And then I always hear His answer: *Don't worry—for THIS you have Me.* He is with us in the darkness just as surely as He is with us in the light. When we trust Him, the dark clouds of trouble are but the shadow of His wings!

> Lord, I just don't understand
> What in the world you're doing in my life.

And back will come His answer:

> *My child, don't try to understand.*
> *Just live it*
> *For me.*

—RUTH HARMS CALKIN

When my heart was sad and I was angry, I was
senseless and stupid. I acted like an animal toward you.
But I am always with you; you have held my hand.
(PSALM 73:21–23 NCV)

It's normal to blame God and be angry at Him for some of our losses. But as our anger cools we can learn a valuable lesson about a monstrous myth—that faith in God is an insurance policy against severe blows in this life. We forget we are living in a broken world with broken lives, broken hearts, broken dreams. Was I mad at God when Tim was killed? Certainly. How unfair, how cruel, how crushing! But lying deep beneath these feelings was my faith that God makes no mistakes. He didn't cause that drunken driver to cross the center line. But I knew nothing ever happens to us that God doesn't know about. Most importantly, I knew God still loved us, and He was there for us in our grief—and in our anger.

The rain falls on the just and also on the unjust . . . but
chiefly on the just, because the unjust steals the just's
umbrella!

October 18

Anyone who answers without listening is foolish and confused. (PROVERBS 18:13 NCV)

"No, dear. The phone's working fine — you just answered the TV remote."

Marriage is like twirling a baton, turning handsprings, or eating with chopsticks. It looks easy until you try it.
—HELEN ROWLAND

October 19

Overlook my youthful sins, O Lord! Look at me instead through eyes of mercy and forgiveness, through eyes of everlasting love and kindness. (PSALM 25:6–7 TLB)

A little boy said to his friend, "Wouldn't you *hate* to wear glasses?"

"No," his friend replied, "not if I could have the kind my grandma wears! My mother says Grandma can always see when folks are tired or discouraged or sad. She sees when somebody is in need, and she can always recognize when you have something on your mind that you need to talk over. But best of all, she can always see something *good* in everybody!"

The little fellow continued, "I asked my grandma one day how it was that she could see that way. She said it was because of the way she's learned to look at things since she's gotten older. So I'm sure it must be those glasses of hers!"

Wouldn't it be wonderful if all of us could see others through Grandma's glasses?

Pour out what you have to enrich the lives of others, and you will soon find your own cup running over with joy.

October 20

Cast your burden upon the LORD, and He will sustain you. (PSALM 55:22 NASB)

I can't make pain go away, but I do recommend the following method for burden casting. It sounds simplistic, but I know it works because it points us toward God.

Write your burden on a scrap of paper—only one per paper. Seal each burden in a separate envelope. Go to a place where you can be alone to pray, then kneel and lift up each envelope with both hands. Tell God your burdens, fears, and doubts—EVERYTHING about this burden, because this is the last time you will speak of it in such detail. You may cry and your arms may hurt, but keep holding up that envelope until the pain in your arms equals the pain in your heart. Then drop your arms and say, "Lord, take it."

On the envelope, write the date and time when you gave your burden to God. Keep the envelope with your treasured things and step out in faith, relying on the knowledge that God has your burden—so you now have hope!

God walks beside me, so I am never alone. God is on my side, so I can never lose.

You husbands must be careful of your wives, being thoughtful of their needs and honoring them as the weaker sex. Remember that you and your wife are partners in receiving God's blessings, and if you don't treat her as you should, your prayers will not get ready answers. (1 PETER 3:7 TLB)

Thoughts on husbands and wives:

Getting a husband is like buying an old house. You don't see it the way it is but the way it's going to be when you get it remodeled.

* * *

Author and pastor Max Lucado says he used to be a "closet slob" with the attitude, "Life is too short to match your socks. Just buy longer pants." Then, he says, he got married!

* * *

Lyndon Johnson said only two things are necessary to keep one's wife happy. One is to let her think she is having her own way. The other is to let her have it.

We started out with nothing, and we still have most of it left.

October 22

They gave up eating and cried out loud, and many of them lay down on rough cloth and ashes to show how sad they were. (ESTHER 4:3 NCV)

"I'm always losing my car keys, my temper, my memory and my patience... so losing weight should be a breeze!"

You can talk to a man about any subject. He won't under-stand, but you can talk to him.

—NELSON'S BIG BOOK OF LAUGHTER

Then they would put their trust in God and would
not forget his deeds but would keep his commands.
(PSALM 78:7)

Dear Barbara,

A friend of mine who is only fifty years old
tells people she is sixty because she looks GREAT
for sixty but AWFUL for fifty. Should I let people
know she is lying?

Peeved in Podunk

Dear Peeved,

There are a couple of Scripture verses on lies
that I get twisted up sometimes . . . but I think it
goes like this: A lie is an abomination to the Lord
but an ever-present help in time of trouble!

Just encourage her by reminding her that some
people never lose their beauty; they merely move
it from their faces into their hearts.

It is bad to suppress laughter. It goes back down and
spreads to your hips.

October 24

Whatever your hand finds to do, do it with your might.
(ECCLESIASTES 9:10 NKJV)

When I was about ten years old, my dad decided I should learn to play the saw—an actual carpenter's saw. If you hold it between your legs and bend it back and forth at just the right angle, you can get a screechy, whining sound out of it using a violin bow—sort of like a sick cat howling on a fence.

Years later, my saw-playing career came back to haunt me when we were at a restaurant celebrating a friend's birthday. While there, he reminded me that the previous year I had promised to play "Happy Birthday" for him on the saw for his next birthday—and, he said, "Tonight's the night!" With that he promptly pulled out a carpenter's saw and a violin bow—right there in the restaurant! So there I sat in the restaurant booth, *wearing a dress*, screeching out "Happy Birthday" for the guest of honor. You can imagine the attention we drew! The whole scene was terribly embarrassing and very immature. And LOTS of fun!

Sometimes I feel like I'm parallel parked in a diagonal universe.

A man with leprosy came to him and begged him on his knees, "If you are willing, you can make me clean." Filled with compassion, Jesus reached out his hand and touched the man. "I am willing," he said. "Be clean!" (MARK 1:40–41)

My friend Sam Butcher, the creator of Precious Moments, shares my concern for the outcast. In a talk Sam gave recently, he noted that lepers of Jesus' era were condemned by their own deadly afflictions, by their friends and family, and by society and the law. Lepers were totally shunned; some people feared to even *look* at a leper.

In the story told in Mark 1, Jesus was surrounded by a crowd of people, all wanting something from Him. Suddenly the crowd parted as the believers scrambled to keep from touching the one lone leper who was courageously making his way toward Jesus. And then Jesus did something astonishing. He reached out and *touched* the man!

A simple touch, but what a difference it made then . . . and what a difference it makes today on your life and mine.

There is no pocket of sin too deep for God's love to cleanse.

October 26

The LORD your God is with you, he is mighty to save.
He will take great delight in you, he will quiet you with
his love, he will rejoice over you with singing.
(ZEPHANIAH 3:17)

Jesus' example shows that serving others with a humble heart doesn't mean we have to do great, extravagant things to do what Jesus would do. Sometimes we can simply touch the untouchable . . . and share God's loving, life-changing grace.

We do God's work because God promises to work in us and through us. What a comfort His promises are!

I will never leave you nor forsake you. (Joshua 1:5)

I will sustain you and rescue you. (Isaiah 46:4)

I will strengthen you and help you. (Isaiah 41:10)

Call to me and I will answer you. (Jeremiah 33:3)

I am your hiding place. I will protect you from trouble and surround you with songs of deliverance. (Psalm 32:7)

God makes a promise, faith believes it, hope anticipates it, patience quietly awaits it. —DRAPER'S BOOK OF QUOTATIONS FOR THE CHRISTIAN WORLD

Behold, thou desirest truth in the inward parts: and in the hidden part thou shalt make me to know wisdom.
(PSALM 51:6 KJV)

Someone sent me a little piece of advice that says, "What I know from having lived a long life is . . . a sense of humor helps. Memory helps. You can get by with one or the other, but when you lose both, you're vegetation!"

As we get older, we're often caught between two malfunctions. Sometimes, as one quipster said:

I KNOW IT ALL. I JUST CAN'T REMEMBER IT ALL AT ONCE!

This comment reminds me of a darling little white-haired lady I met in Texas. At one point someone asked her a question, and she paused, blinked a few times, and raised an index finger to her lips in an effort to remember the answer. Finally, she said, "Do you need to know right now, or could you wait a little while?"

My only advice (and look who's giving it!) is to hang on to your sense of humor, even as you lose your grip on reality.

I'm not confused. I'm just well-mixed.

October 28

Riches will not help when it's time to die, but right living will save you from death. (PROVERBS 11:4 NCV)

A friend wrote me a wonderful letter that said, "I guess I'm in the golden years. I try to keep an upbeat attitude and laugh a lot. Sometimes I don't remember what I'm laughing about, but it must have been funny, so I keep on. It seems memory loss is a big factor in growing older. The neat thing is that my friends are all in the same boat, so their feelings won't be hurt when I forget because they don't remember either! If I do something stupid, I won't remember long enough to stay embarrassed."

I keep thinking I've forgotten something...

Sign on harried shopkeeper's door: *"Out of my mind. Be back in five minutes."*

Rejoice with those who rejoice, and weep with those who weep. . . . Associate with the humble. Do not be wise in your own opinion. (ROMANS 12:15–16 NKJV)

Recently I read someone's comment that "happiness is a talent." And right after that, I came upon philosopher William James's advice that said, "If you want a quality, act as if you already have it." Even if you think you don't have a talent for happiness, *act* as if you do. You'll find that joy is like a vaccine that immunizes you against all sorts of maladies. Joy opens our hearts to see God's power at work in ourselves and in our world.

Now, no one expects you to make a radical change in attitude all at once. If you're like me, you'll want to taper off your whining gradually so you don't get attitude whiplash! And be aware that there *are* some people out there in the emotional tundra who just can't stand to think of anything or anyone being joyful. It's like that old joke that defined Puritanism as "the haunting fear that someone, somewhere, may be happy."

I've kept a stiff upper lip so long it feels like rigor mortis has set in!

October 30

Look after each other so that not one of you will fail to find God's best blessings. (Hebrews 12:15 TLB)

A young man noticed that an elderly couple sitting down to lunch at McDonald's had ordered just one meal and an extra drink cup. As he watched, the gentleman carefully divided the hamburger in half then counted out the fries, one for him, one for her, until each had half. Next he poured half the soft drink into the extra cup and set that in front of his wife. The old man then began to eat while his wife sat watching, her hands folded demurely in her lap.

The young man gently asked if they would allow him to purchase another meal for them so they didn't have to split theirs. "Oh, no," the old gentleman replied. "We've been married sixty years, and everything has always been fifty-fifty."

Then the young man asked the wife if she was going to eat. "Not yet," she replied. "It's his turn with the teeth."

This is a rule for women that has no exceptions: *If it has tires or testosterone, you're gonna have trouble with it!*

*How beautiful you are, my love. . . . Your hair falls across your face like flocks of goats that frisk across the slopes of Gilead. (*Song of Solomon 4:1 tlb*)*

We all felt sorry for the front desk clerk when the Women of Faith speakers checked into our Charlotte hotel. Her eyes sparkled so merrily, and she seemed constantly about to burst into laughter. But she was *very* pregnant, and—oh, dear!—she had a *very* noticeable facial-hair problem: a thin, black mustache that was easily visible from across the lobby. We even thought about offering her an electrolysis scholarship but couldn't figure out how to do it without hurting her feelings. Three days later, as I checked out of the hotel, there was something about *that* desk clerk too. He was a handsome young man with sparkly eyes, a bright smile—and good grief! That same mustache the pregnant woman had had on Thursday! I was flabbergasted. "You—you . . . on Thursday, you . . . ?"

"That was me, all right," he said with a chuckle. "The hotel was having a costume contest for Halloween, and I won first prize!"

Laughter has no foreign accent.

November 1

Just as you received Christ Jesus as Lord, continue to live in him, rooted and built up in him, strengthened in the faith as you were taught, and overflowing with thankfulness. (COLOSSIANS 2:6–7)

Happy November! This month we celebrate *thankfulness.* November is a time to count our many blessings—name them one by one. It's always amazing to me, reading the agony that pours out of my mail every day, to find signs of thankfulness too. Here's a tiny sampling:

> "Our son has not solved his personal problems, but we have reconciled. He phones occasionally from faraway places. . . . For this we are thankful."

* * *

> "Thank You, Lord, for what You are doing in the life of our son, even though we cannot see it now."

* * *

> "Barbara, thank you for letting me see your scars . . . for now I know there is hope for me also. Even though I am in the tunnel, I know there will be light again."

Why do the Pilgrims' pants keep falling down? *Because they wear their belts around their hats!*

Do not be anxious about anything, but in everything,
by prayer and petition, with thanksgiving, present your
requests to God. And the peace of God, which transcends
all understanding, will guard your hearts and your
minds in Christ Jesus. (PHILIPPIANS 4:6–7)

The happiest marriages are surely those where love and laughter overcome any brokenness. Between these couples, laughter is a natural part of every day. What a blessing! A friend sent me a packet of funny tidbits and said she had hoped to send a photocopy of her favorite cartoon, entitled "The Incurable Romantic," as well. But she couldn't copy it, because her husband had *glued* it inside the medicine cabinet door. Instead she had to describe it to me: The illustration showed a man climbing into bed with his wife and saying, "The light reflected off your night cream is like moonlight on a still mountain pool, and the silver gleam of curlers under the hair net suggests dew on cobwebs in some remote glade."

Can't you just see that husband and wife, chuckling every morning when they open the medicine cabinet to reach for the toothpaste?

Always laugh when you can. It is cheap medicine.

November 3

And God will wipe away every tear from their eyes.
(REVELATION 7:17)

It was during our son Steve's memorial service that I moved from shock and denial into the next stage of grief—suffering. For me, the tears were a continuing catharsis that helped wash away my denial. They helped me face the fact that Steve was gone.

Bill mourned a different way. He was as grief-stricken as I was, but he refused to weep during the service. He had done that earlier at home, pounding on the armrest of his rocking chair and muttering, "HOW could it happen? He was so YOUNG . . ."

Our grief was different, but we shared a common belief that brought us both comfort. We could still feel secure because we knew Steve was safe in the arms of Jesus. He was our "deposit in heaven," and I was comforted to remember:

Death is not extinguishing the light. It is putting out the lamp because the dawn has come.

Don't let the sun go down with you still angry—get over it quickly; for when you are angry you give a mighty foothold to the devil. (EPHESIANS 4:26–27 TLB)

When my shock turned into pain after our son Tim was killed by a drunken driver, anger immediately welled up within me. When I share my story of going to the dump to rant and rave at God, many parents tell me they feel relieved because they, too, have been mad at God after a loved one's death. How thankful I am that, when we rage at Him through our grief, He doesn't say, "Off to hell with you, sister!" Instead, He patiently loves us . . . and carries us . . . wraps His blanket of tenderness around us while we are balking, hissing, and rebelling in every way.

You see, God gave us our emotions. We are made in God's image, and throughout the Old Testament we see God sometimes becoming angry! Anger induced by pain and grief is a normal response to deep hurt. It is one of the ways we ventilate our feelings so that healing can begin.

For every minute you are angry, you lose sixty seconds of happiness.

November 5

Has your heart carried you away from God? Why do your eyes flash with anger? (JOB 15:12 NCV)

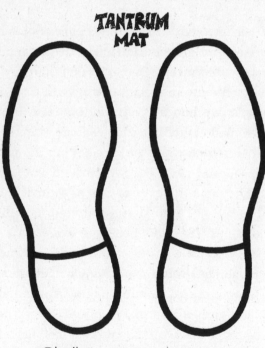

TANTRUM MAT

Directions: —
When the need for throwing a tantrum is felt, place both feet on the space provided and jump rapidly up and down. Incoherent screaming is also permissible. If symptoms persist, see your nearest psychiatrist — You MAY be a nut.

He poured water into a basin and began to wash the disciples' feet, and to wipe them with the towel with which He was girded. (JOHN 13:5 NKJV)

If we were royal heirs to an earthly monarch, we might have grand, attention-getting duties such as leading military campaigns or reigning over lavish cere-monial affairs. Instead, we are heirs to a servant King, whom we honor by serving others in humility and in love. Our duty here may be something simple . . . and even more important:

- To speak a healing word to a broken heart.

- To extend a hand to one who has fallen.

- To give a smile to those whose laughter has been lost.

- To encourage the dreamer who has given up.

- To ease the burden of one bent low beneath a thankless task.

- To reassure the doubter and reinforce the believer.

- To light the candle of God's Word in the midst of another's darkest night.

Kindness is love in work clothes. —DRAPER'S BOOK OF QUOTATIONS FOR THE CHRISTIAN WORLD

November 7

God is love. Those who live in love live in God, and God lives in them. (1 JOHN 4:16 NCV)

Our heavenly crowns may be glorious ornaments we'll wear while singing praises to our King when we get to heaven, but here on earth, Christ's crown of servanthood should come with a chin strap, because we have a lot of work to do! A woman sent me an essay recently that describes the "doodles" that appear on her friend's prayer journal. One of the drawings is a crown, drawn there to remind her, as she prays for her children, that "what they are today is not what they will be tomorrow." The same is true for all of us. And it just may be that WE are the instruments He's using to love or encourage someone else.

"Oh, how I wish the Lord would come during my lifetime!" Queen Victoria of England told one of her advisers. When he asked why, she replied, "Because I would love to lay my crown at His blessed feet in reverent adoration."

—*THE SPEAKER'S QUOTE BOOK*

I will see the rainbow in the cloud and remember my
eternal promise to every living being on the earth.
(GENESIS 9:16–17 TLB)

L ife storms buffet us, ripping apart our plans and flooding us with multiplied problems. But grace is God's promise that we will not be destroyed, just as a rainbow was His promise that He would never again send a flood to devastate the earth.

Phyllis Eger tells a lovely story about how a phone call interrupted her dinner preparations as a neighbor told her to hurry outside to see the most beautiful rainbow in the eastern sky. She turned off her stove and dashed outside, and there it was—a spectacular double arc of lovely colors. She quickly called her mother who lived across town, and her mother, in turn, called a neighbor. Other families saw them looking up at the sky and came out to see what was going on. Soon more than a dozen people were appreciating that beautiful rainbow—all because one lady made a phone call.

The soul would have no rainbows if the eyes had no tears.

November 9

Happy are they whose sins are forgiven.
(ROMANS 4:7 NCV)

Parents suffer all sorts of emotional responses when they land on the ceiling. When I learned about Larry's homosexuality, I was flooded with guilt as well as physical symptoms that included itchy teeth and what felt like a shag rug in my throat. Recently I met another mother who completely lost all of her hair within a week of learning her son was gay. When she pulled off the scarf she was wearing, there were only some fine, downy patches of sparse hair, sort of like hamster hair.

I tried to help her, reminding her that the way our kids turn out is really not under our control. But I had no idea if she could ever regrow her hair. Then, a few months later, she called and, in a cheery voice, asked, "Remember the lady with the hamster hair?" She said her hair had grown back in and she was off to get a permanent!

Hair can grow out, stomach pains can stop, and hearts can be mended . . . with:

The three ingredients of recovery: Tears, Talking, and TIME!

Take a new grip with your tired hands, stand firm on your shaky legs, and mark out a straight, smooth path for your feet so that those who follow you, though weak and lame, will not fall and hurt themselves, but become strong. (HEBREWS 12:12–13 TLB)

Dear Barbara,

I, too, began my grief by counting the roses on the bedroom wallpaper. Then one day, I took one second out of my counting and smiled at myself in the mirror. I added one second of smiling into the mirror every day until I was really smiling again, outside and inside. Here are some other steps I took from your books: (1) Cried. (2) Moved toward happiness. (3) Started a Joy Box with small stuff. (4) Started a Joy ROOM with big stuff. (5) Gave myself a party. (It made me happy to see others happy.) (6) Helped a friend and let her lean on me. (7) Sought help. A listening ear is crucial, even if it is a paid ear. (8) Typed out what I underlined in your books. (9) Prayed / Bible study. (10) Thanked God even for sand-grain-size blessings.

Still water runs deep . . . when the toilet overflows.

November 11

*The centurion replied, "Lord, I do not deserve to have
you come under my roof. But just say the word, and my
servant will be healed. For I myself am a man under
authority, with soldiers under me. . . ." When Jesus heard
this, he was astonished and said . . . "I tell you the truth,
I have not found anyone in Israel with such great faith."*
(MATTHEW 8:8–10)

On Veterans Day, I think of the veterans in my
life—my husband, Bill, of course, and two of our
four sons—Steve, a marine killed in Vietnam, and Tim,
who served with the air force before he was killed by a
drunk driver. Both were buried with military honors,
and one scene stands out in that teary blur of memories.
At the graveside, the honor guard precisely folded the
flag covering Steven's casket. Then, before he handed it
respectfully to Bill, the leader of the honor guard gently
touched the folded flag to his heart—a tiny gesture that
has comforted me for nearly thirty years.

Remembering that moment, I realize we never know
who or how others will be affected by the simplest gesture of kindness we share.

There is nothing small in the service of God.

"God has made me laugh. Everyone who hears about this will laugh with me." [—Sarah, aged wife of one-hundred-year-old Abraham, upon the birth of their son, Isaac] (GENESIS 21:5–6 NCV)

"Having nine lives is cool, but if I have to go through menopause again, forget it!"

Thirty is the ideal age for a woman—especially if she's forty. —NELSON'S BIG BOOK OF LAUGHTER

November 13

Better a dry crust with peace and quiet than a house full of feasting, with strife. (PROVERBS 17:1)

How to know it's time to diet:

- You take a shower and nothing below your waist gets wet.

- You get a pedicure and have to look in a mirror to see what color the manicurist painted your toenails.

- You get out of breath just blinking your eyes in bright sunlight.

- Your finger gets stuck in the holes of dial telephones.

- Tollbooth operators suggest that next time you use the lane marked "WIDE LOADS."

- On hot days, small children flock to you to stay in the shade.

- Bus drivers ask you to sit up front to serve as an air bag for the rest of the passengers in case of a crash.

There are only two things you need to avoid in order to lose weight: *food and drink!*

*For you have delivered me from death and my feet from
stumbling, that I may walk before God in the light of life.*
(PSALM 56:13)

When we're able to relinquish ALL our problems, ALL our worries, and ALL our sins to the
Lord, we are free to live the guilt-free lives He planned
for us. God can help you find the SONshine inside
yourself so you can laugh again. No matter where you
are, He is with you, and as someone said: *I would rather
walk with God in the dark than go alone in the light.*

One mother wrote me to say, "Each of us is in various stages of recovery from WHATEVER, and it's
important that we are able to laugh along the way. It's
kept me from insanity numerous times. . . . Out of your
heartache comes something beautiful that God has
used, is using, or *will* use."

**It's no longer a question of staying healthy. It's a ques-
tion of finding a sickness you like.** —JACKIE MASON

November 15

Children's children are a crown to the aged, and parents are the pride of their children. (PROVERBS 17:6)

Supergranny

Don't look for her in the rocking chair;
Granny isn't in it.
She's off to fight a fire somewhere
Or serving in the Senate

She might be in a cockpit
Or removing an appendix
Or checking test tubes in a lab
Or speaking from a pulpit.

She could be on a book tour
Or working as a chef.
Or running a big company
From behind a corporate desk.

A lot has changed in granny's world;
She studies to keep up.
But one thing still comes natural:
That special Granny LOVE!

—ANN LUNA

She who kneels before God can stand before anybody.

Correct your children while there is still hope; do not let them destroy themselves. (PROVERBS 19:18 NCV)

In an effort to prepare expectant parents for the challenges that lie ahead, many obstetricians' offices have installed parenthood simulators.

Child's advice: *If you want a kitten, start by asking for a pony.*

Whenever he entered the LORD's presence to speak with him, he removed the veil until he came out. And when he came out and told the Israelites what he had been commanded, they saw that his face was radiant.
(EXODUS 34:34–35)

When I was at the NBC studios in Burbank, California, to tape a television show, I sat in the makeup chair looking at a big mirror surrounded by those bright, merciless lights. A sign placed just above the mirror proclaimed in huge black letters:

IF YOU WANT MAKEUP, ASK ME.
IF YOU WANT MIRACLES, ASK GOD.

When you're looking in the mirror, it's always good to remember some of the Bible's "I am" verses:

1. A child of God (Romans 8:16)
2. Forgiven (Colossians 1:13–14)
3. Saved by grace through faith (Ephesians 2:8)
4. Casting all my cares on Jesus (1 Peter 5:7)
5. Filled with laughter and rejoicing (Job 8:21)

The great beautifier is a contented heart and a happy outlook.

Someone who is laughing may be sad inside.
(PROVERBS 14:13 NCV)

A darling mom who is part of one of our support groups once told me, "Spatula Ministries is a very elite bunch. It's a club where not many are willing to pay the initiation fee to become a member!"

She smiled when she said it, and I smiled back, knowing she was right. The initiation fee to become a "Spatula-lander" is suffering. Sooner or later, we all wind up with our grief work to do. Understanding grief is a complicated process. Why do some folks recover after suffering a terrible loss while others do not? Those who get better *have done their grief work.*

Grief work should be done in an atmosphere of healthy dependency. Don't go into isolation! In your condition, you need to be nurtured. Don't be afraid to let others help you. When you are grieving, you cannot think clearly. Grief work is what friends are for.

When you're in a jam, good friends will bring you bread with peanut butter on it.

November 19

He has also set eternity in the hearts of men; yet they
cannot fathom what God has done from beginning to end.
(ECCLESIASTES 3:11)

THE FAMILY CIRCUS By Bil Keane

"If somebody dies in the hospital,
angels move them to the
eternity ward."

Pity the poor guy who bought a cemetery plot—then took
a cruise and was lost at sea. —NORM CROSBY

In You, O LORD, I put my trust. . . . For You are my hope, O Lord GOD; You are my trust from my youth. (PSALM 71:1, 5 NKJV)

So many parents write or call me and ask, "How can we give our kids to God and find some relief for this devastation we feel?" I believe, from my own struggling, that each of us must go through those *stages* of relinquishment: CHURN awhile . . . BURN for a time . . . YEARN for as long as it takes to move on . . . LEARN as much as you can . . . and then TURN it all over to the One who cares for you. Don't fret if you think you're not progressing or even when suddenly, for no reason, you find yourself back at square one, churning, just as you did at the beginning. That is normal and very typical of grief. Never forget this is a grief *process,* and it is *work!* The mending process takes time, but you are making a long journey to becoming whole again, and you have a *door of hope* ahead.

Hope is faith holding out its hands in the dark.

—GEORGE ILES

November 21

Let the peace that Christ gives control your thinking, because you were all called together in one body to have peace. Always be thankful. (COLOSSIANS 3:15 NCV)

In this season of thanksgiving, let us be grateful . . .

- For husbands who attack small repair jobs around the house. They usually make them big enough to call in professionals.

- For children who put away their things and clean up after themselves. They're such a joy you hate to see them go home to their own parents.

During all the hustle-bustle of the holiday season, don't forget to schedule some time for laughter. A good cry is a wet-wash, but a hearty laugh gives you a dry cleaning. It is worth a hundred groans anytime in any market. Truly, laughter is the sun that drives winter from the human face.

A keen sense of humor helps us to overlook the unbecoming, understand the unconventional, tolerate the unpleasant, overcome the unexpected, and outlast the unbearable.

To those who are weak, I became weak so I could win the weak. I have become all things to all people so I could save some of them in any way possible. I do all this because of the Good News and so I can share in its blessings.
(1 CORINTHIANS 9:22–23 NCV)

It has been said that joy is the flag you fly when the Prince of Peace resides in your heart. Our responsibility as Christians is to be contagious! Here are some suggestions for spreading your joy:

- Pray that the Holy Spirit will fill you with His joy.

- Write to some joy-poor friends and enclose cartoons or humorous clippings. Give others sincere praise and warm encouragement. Remember that *encourage* means "to fill the heart." Take some time to fill another's heart and see how that goodness will boomerang back to fill your own.

- Seek out some joy-giving friends to refresh your battered spirit.

- Finally, become a joy germ and infect everyone around you!

You can only be young once, but you can be immature forever.

November 23

Let the teaching of Christ live in you richly. Use all wisdom to teach and instruct each other by singing psalms, hymns, and spiritual songs with thankfulness in your hearts to God. (COLOSSIANS 3:16 NCV)

Truly, we are very rich people—and what better time than the season of Thanksgiving to sit back and count our blessings. Sure, our hearts have been broken and our minds have been run through the wringer, but as Christians we have incredible wealth, bought for us at an unimaginable price. So how do we manage that wealth? We live joyously, sharing the good news wherever we go. I love the little verse that says, "Two eyes to look at God above, two hands to clasp in prayer, two feet to carry me to church—that's why I'm a MILLIONAIRE!"

Share the wealth of blessings you've received: *Every day, go out of your way to do something kind for someone.*

Live happily with the woman you love through the fleeting days of life, for the wife God gives you is your best reward down here for all your earthly toil.
(ECCLESIASTES 9:9 TLB)

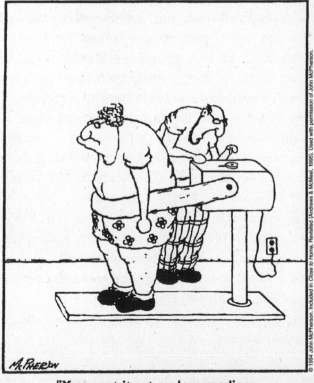

"You want it set on low, medium,
or high or industrial strength?"

November 25

For Christ's sake, I delight in weaknesses, in insults, in hardships, in persecutions, in difficulties. For when I am weak, then I am strong. (2 CORINTHIANS 12:10)

Thank heaven Joni Eareckson Tada was with us in California when, due to a misunderstanding, the Women of Faith conference was seriously oversold. As a result, hundreds of disgruntled women were assigned to hard, narrow folding chairs, watching the conference on television monitors in the basement! Fortunately the ever-joyful Joni was the first speaker that night. She wheeled out onto the stage. "I hear some of you aren't too happy with your chairs tonight," she said, smiling warmly. "I certainly understand your feelings. I *hate* my chair!"

There was a little collective gasp as Joni's words sank in while all eyes took in the sight of her frail, slim body strapped into the wheelchair. "And you know what? I have thousands of friends who would *gladly* change chairs with you right now."

Suddenly the tension was eased . . . and twenty thousand women had a new perspective.

Success is not measured by how high you fly but how high you bounce.

How great is the love the Father has lavished on us, that we should be called children of God! (1 JOHN 3:1)

Being a grandmother means we have a special opportunity to give unfailing, unquestioning, nonjudgmental, nonstop, full-powered love to our grandchildren. And while it's true that giving children too many material things can be detrimental, it's absolutely impossible to give a child too much love. As someone said:

Extra love from grandparents goes into a child's psychological bank account, which draws interest and can be used for an emotionally rainy day.

What a comforting thought—to imagine our grandchildren facing some tough decision someday or feeling lonely in some far-off place and suddenly remembering a grandmother's love—and being comforted by it. Surely there's no greater legacy we can leave them than this enduring gift—the kind of love modeled by Jesus. Love that never ends.

Children certainly brighten up a home. Whoever saw a child under twelve turn off an electric light?

November 27

He will keep in perfect peace all those who trust in him,
whose thoughts turn often to the Lord! (ISAIAH 26:3 TLB)

The other night I sat in a restaurant parking lot until 2 A.M. helping a young man dying of AIDS plan his funeral. It was too difficult for his parents, and I felt honored that he wanted me to help make plans for what he knew was coming. Afterward, I came home, drained, and as I watched a Scripture video, I felt God's Word replenishing my joy.

When speaking to women's groups, I say, "You may think you have it altogether, but then something will come along to remind you that you NEVER have it altogether. The older you get, the more experienced you are, the more you realize that you get one wall up and the other wall falls down. If it's not a physical problem, it'll be emotional or mental. The point is that *you have to accept what life hands you.* The stress will always be there, but God will always be there, too, and that helps you survive!"

Worry is wasting today's time to clutter up tomorrow's opportunities with yesterday's troubles.

Do not think of yourself more highly than you ought.
(ROMANS 12:3)

One time at traffic school I somehow ended up in a class of motorcyclists who, like me, were attending to keep their traffic tickets off their driving records. Everywhere I looked I saw red bandannas, grubby beards, sleeveless T-shirts sporting vulgar phrases, tattoos that were even more vulgar, leather jackets, and heavy boots. I sat between two huge, bearded bikers who made the words "incredible hulk" come to mind. The windowless room was hot, the air conditioning wasn't working, and the odor was a cross between a pig farm and a glue factory. I was delighted to get my certificate late that afternoon and escape.

That night I was describing the biker crowd to Bill in gory detail when I thought I heard the Savior's voice whispering in my mind: "You know, Barbara, I died for *them* as well as for *you*." I winced and said a quick prayer for my classmates—especially the one with swastikas on his helmet.

If we ever make a mistake in judgment, let it be on the side of mercy.

November 29

He who overcomes shall thus be clothed in white garments; and I will not erase his name from the book of life, and I will confess his name before My Father, and before His angels. (REVELATION 3:5 NASB)

When we do angel work in Jesus' name, we demonstrate His love to others. These kindnesses don't have to be daring or costly. An encouraging word—or simply an attitude of joy—can make the difference to someone who's given up hope. A little smile can brighten someone's day. And while you're smiling you might as well go one step further and share a chuckle or two. After all, a laugh is just a smile with a soundtrack.

C. S. Lewis said, "The best argument for Christianity is Christians: their joy, their certainty, their completeness." Lewis also warned, however, that Christians can be "the strongest argument *against* Christianity . . . when they are somber and joyless, when they are self-righteous and smug, . . . when they are narrow and repressive."

Let's resolve to be angels of joy and missionaries of mirth wherever we go today—and every day!

A Christian is a living sermon.

*You will not be afraid of diseases that come in the dark or
sickness that strikes at noon.* (PSALM 91:6 NCV)

A fellow who was prone to motion sickness
crowded onto a subway train on his way home
from work. He had eaten a big lunch and had worked
all afternoon with an upset stomach. The longer he
rode the speeding, swaying train, the sicker he got.
Finally the train screeched to a stop, but it wasn't the
sick man's stop. Several people were on the platform,
waiting to get on. The train stopped, the doors opened,
and suddenly OUT CAME THE MAN'S LUNCH—all
over a guy waiting to get on the train! The poor man
just stood there in shocked outrage. Before anyone
could move, the doors shut, the train went on, and
there stood the man on the platform, covered with
another man's lunch, and whining, "WHY ME?"

That's how lots of us hurting parents feel when life
throws us for a loop. But eventually we learn to replace
"Why me?" with "Whatever, Lord!" Then we know
we're on the track toward HOME.

*If you're headed in the wrong direction, God allows
U-turns.*

December 1

> *"The virgin will be pregnant. She will have a son, and they will name him Immanuel," which means "God is with us."* (MATTHEW 1:23 NCV)

And now the *real* celebrating begins! On December 1, with both joy and trepidation, we begin focusing on the biggest event of the year: Christmas! We're joyful, because we're celebrating the birth of our Lord. And, for families who have lost a loved one, we're fearful, because grief often intensifies during the holidays. Too easily, you may feel yourself dissolving into a whirlpool of helplessness. But keep clinging to Jesus, and keep repeating this rule: Pain is inevitable in this life, but misery is OPTIONAL! You still have a choice about how you respond to the heartache that threatens to turn your world upside down. In December . . . and in *every circumstance*—choose JOY!

My favorite way to offset holiday stress: *Lie on your back and eat celery, using your navel as a salt dipper.*

It is hard to find a good wife, because she is worth more than rubies. . . . She is like a trader's ship, bringing food from far away. (PROVERBS 31:10, 14 NCV)

This cartoon by my friend Dana Summers is dedicated to all of you weary holiday shoppers!

Church Bulletin Blooper: *Offertory Solo: "O Holy Nighty"*

December 3

*God gives some people the ability . . . to accept their state
in life and enjoy their work. They do not worry about
how short life is, because God keeps them busy with what
they love to do.* (ECCLESIASTES 5:19–20 NCV)

Our firstborn son, Tim, was a serious, conscientious kid who had a different sense of humor than the rest of us. His idea of something hilarious was to bring home the bows from the funeral home where he worked. Later our dogs would show up wearing "REST IN PEACE" or "GOD BLESS GRANDPA HIRAM" on bows around their necks.

One day Tim took his little brother, Barney, to the mortuary. When no one was around, Tim let Barney climb into an empty casket just to see what it felt like. Then (just for fun) Tim shut the lid! Barney let out a yelp, and Tim opened the lid—after he'd had a good laugh, of course.

The next day during circle time at Barney's school, Barney shared what had happened. Barney's teacher called me later to say, "Mrs. Johnson, I'm afraid Barney is starting to tell lies. He's coming up with stories that just *can't* be true!"

Life is what happens after you make other plans.

Fix your thoughts on what is true and good and right.
Think about things that are pure and lovely, and dwell
on the fine, good things in others. Think about all you
can praise God for and be glad about it.
(PHILIPPIANS 4:8 TLB)

Over the years I've learned ways to find splashes of joy when life turns into a cesspool. One way is through Philippians 4:8, the verse I call my "rubbish-removal service." It's the verse I use to dump the garbage from my mind and get rid of useless, rotting, noxious junk so I can replace it with thoughts that are nourishing, fresh, and healthy. A lot has been written on "positive thinking," but Paul scooped everybody two thousand years ago with Philippians 4:8, which he wrote in prison chained to a Roman guard, waiting to be executed. In a JOY-*LESS* place, in JOY-*LESS* circumstances, Paul was JOY-*FULL* because he knew that the difference between splashes of joy and the cesspool often depends on how we look at what is happening to us.

A smile is a wrinkle that shouldn't be removed. It is the
lighting system of the face and the heating system of
the heart.

December 5

[Jesus said,] "Blessed are those who don't doubt me."
(MATTHEW 11:6 TLB)

Hope is the essential ingredient to make it through life. It is the anchor of the soul. When you quit depending on your own strength to solve your problems, that's when you can start to have REAL hope in what God can do! Think of your life with all the mistakes, sins, and woes of the past like the tangles in a ball of yarn, knotted up with "whys?" and endless loops of frustration. Especially during the holidays, it may become such a mess that you could never begin to straighten it out. God alone can untangle the threads of our lives. What a comfort it is to drop the tangles of life into God's hands and then *leave them there.* That's what hope is all about.

If people love me, they will obey my teaching. My Father will love them, and we will come to them and make our home with them. (JOHN 14:23 NCV)

Whatever you and your house are like—whether your housekeeping system is the casual stow-and-slam method or the super-organized home where even the dustballs line up evenly under the bed, the most important thing to fill your home with is *joy*. What a blessing it is to step inside a home and immediately feel surrounded by a bubble of laughter and a blanket of love. In my home, I've tried to make the colors blend and the furniture fit. But the most important thing is that wherever I look in our house, I see things that bring a smile to my face and warmth to my heart.

Winston Churchill said, "We make a living by what we get. We make a LIFE by what we GIVE." What have you given lately?

December 7

I cried like a bird and moaned like a dove. My eyes became tired as I looked to the heavens. LORD, I have troubles. Please help me. (ISAIAH 38:14 NCV)

Holidays come equipped with stress, but keep reminding yourself that you WILL survive. When stress overwhelms me, I try to focus on the wonderfully relaxed future Jesus has promised us when we will live in heaven in peace with Him and there will be no more stress or pain.

Experts say that exercising and soaking in a warm bath are two great stress-relievers. But here's my favorite: laughing. A medical expert once said, "Laughing for twenty seconds . . . gives the body the kind of workout you'd get from three minutes of rigorous rowing." Now THAT'S a holiday gift I can use! The professor suggested that when stressed-out people arrive home from work or holiday shopping, they try to walk in with a funny story to share instead of a complaint. "And be on the lookout for the kinds of experiences that are not only funny (and relaxing) when they happen but will make good stories later."

Can it be an accident that "STRESSED" is "DESSERTS" spelled backward?

*And there were in the same country shepherds abiding
in the field, keeping watch over their flock by night.*
(LUKE 2:8 KJV)

When Larry was ten he was assigned a solo,
"While Shepherds Watched Their Flocks by
Night," in a church Christmas program. I helped him
practice, and sometimes he'd get silly and sing, "While
shepherds washed their socks by night all seated on
the ground, the angel of the Lord came down and said,
'Will you wash mine?'"

We were kidding around one day when Larry kept
singing it the wrong way, just to get me laughing.
Finally I offered to give him five dollars if he would
sing it that way at church. Larry laughed and said he
wouldn't, of course, but on the night of the program he
either forgot or changed his mind! He got out there in
front of all the people and started singing, "While
shepherds washed their socks by night . . ."

Instead of being shocked, the audience got tickled,
and soon everybody was laughing and clapping. The
fun we had that night—and since then, remembering—was well worth the money!

God gave us memories so we could have roses in December.

December 9

If you believe, you will get anything you ask for in prayer. (MATTHEW 21:22 NCV)

A thought to help you through the holidays with laughter:

> The Four Stages of Life
>
> 1. You believe in Santa Claus.
>
> 2. You don't believe in Santa Claus.
>
> 3. You are Santa Claus.
>
> 4. You look like Santa Claus.

What other time of year do you sit in front of a dead tree in the living room and eat candy out of your socks?

*First, there is nothing better for a man than to be happy
and to enjoy himself as long as he can; and second, that
he should eat and drink and enjoy the fruits of his labors,
for these are gifts from God.* (ECCLESIASTES 3:12–13 TLB)

For Sale—*Complete twenty-five-volume set of encyclopedia. Latest edition, never used. Wife knows everything.*

December 11

And she brought forth her firstborn Son, and wrapped
Him in swaddling cloths, and laid Him in a manger,
because there was no room for them in the inn.
(LUKE 2:7 NKJV)

Little Andy was miffed when he didn't get the part he wanted in the Sunday school Christmas pageant. He had hoped for the role of Joseph, but instead got stuck being the innkeeper. He decided to pull a fast one and get even.

As scheduled, Mary and Joseph came to his place seeking shelter. "Come right in, folks. I've got plenty of room," he said.

Perplexed, the children playing Mary and Joseph didn't know what to do as he showed them around his inn. Then Joseph, equal to the occasion, said to Mary, "Hey, this place is a dump. I'd rather go out and sleep in the stable."

'Tis the season to be chubby.

Our hope is in the LORD. He is our help, our shield to protect us. (PSALM 33:20 NCV)

Dr. Karl Menninger, the world-famous psychiatrist, was answering questions after giving a lecture on mental health when one person asked, "What would you advise someone to do if he felt a nervous breakdown coming on?"

Most people expected the doctor to say, "Consult a psychiatrist." Instead he said, "Lock up your house, go across the railroad tracks, find someone in need, and do something to help that person."

Many hurting parents have found a way to share joy during the holidays by volunteering in homeless shelters, soup kitchens, or doing other volunteer activities. The important thing is not to mope around, waiting for an invitation—get out there and find someone who's even worse off than you are, or invite a lonely person to share a holiday meal with you.

Heed a lesson from man's best friend: When someone is having a bad day, be silent, sit close by, and nuzzle them.

December 13

Great peace have they who love your law, and nothing can make them stumble. (PSALM 119:165)

Consider these steps for reducing stress and sadness during the holidays:

- Accept the fact that you ARE stressed and depressed while the rest of the world seems merry.

- Tell yourself this is NOT a permanent thing. It too will pass.

- Set a deadline for your dark days to end. Tell yourself that on that date you will put your sadness behind you and step out in joy.

- Set priorities, and practice saying no. Don't be afraid to change traditions if you can't cope with doing things the old way.

- Be gentle with yourself. Spend time with people who love, support, and accept you as you are.

- Take time out from the hustle and bustle to be alone with God—your hope, your strength, and your promise of a brighter tomorrow.

Grief can be your servant, helping you to feel more compassion for others who hurt.

I will not forget you. See, I have inscribed you on the palms of My hands. (ISAIAH 49:15–16 NKJV)

The blessings that come from reaching out to others cannot be overestimated. I learn this anew every year around Christmas. We usually have several dozen families who have lost a loved one during the year, either from AIDS, suicide, or some other tragedy. So over the years I have started around December 14 (my birthday in case you want to send me a present!), and I set aside everything else and start telephoning the families who have experienced a loss.

Usually when I get them on the phone it takes a minute for them to connect ME with the person who writes the books. Then they call another person to the phone, and soon every phone in the house has a family member talking. They appreciate that someone cared enough to remember their loss at holiday time. Their reaction proves the truth of that adage:

People don't care how much you know. They just need to know how much you care.

December 15

Whatever you do, work at it with all your heart, as working for the Lord, not for men. (COLOSSIANS 3:23)

It is a real effort to make those calls at Christmas time, but soon the splashes of joy that boomerang back to me fill me with so much love, *my heart smiles*. I can't help but share their excitement in knowing someone really CARES about their feelings when their loss is still so fresh.

I love to remind them that GOD IS STILL IN CHARGE OF IT ALL. Then I pray with them and ask God to wrap His comfort blanket around them and grant them His peace. Somehow the idea of being wrapped in God's blanket of love reminds them they are contained in His care—and not splattered all over the ceiling.

Making these calls is a boomerang joy that comes back as my personal Christmas gift to myself. I know when there's been a loss—whether it's caused by illness, death, estrangement, moving, or whatever—holidays can easily bring more heaviness instead of happiness for those who are already depressed.

At yuletide, the best holiday decoration is to be wreathed in smiles.

*You hear, O LORD, the desire of the afflicted; you
encourage them, and you listen to their cry.*
(PSALM 10:17)

ven a *little* affirmation can bring us the greatest
results. I thought of that recently when Bill and
I stayed in a lovely old bed-and-breakfast place. It was
furnished with lots of antique things for us to examine
and enjoy. In our room, we found a contraption made
of a long wooden stick with a bellows sort of thing at
one end. It was hanging beside the bed, and when I
asked the hostess about it, she said it was a *quilt fluffer*.
When you slid it inside the covers and worked the bellows, it blew puffs of air between the quilts to fluff
them up, making them as light as a feather. What a difference it made to snuggle into those fluffed-up covers!

*One of the ways we share God's love is through encour-
agement. The word* **encourage** *means "to fill the heart, to
puff it up, to enlarge it." By encouraging a friend, we give
that person a special, heart-felt gift.*

December 17

Fear and trembling have beset me; horror has
overwhelmed me. I said, "Oh, that I had the wings of a
dove! I would fly away and be at rest." (PSALM 55:5–6)

During the hectic holiday season, it's sometimes encouraging just to be told we're not going crazy when we feel ourselves slipping over the brink into La-La Land. That's what a hospice nurse did when she reminded a grieving woman that the stress of simply trying to survive her loss might cause her to do "crazy things." The nurse told the woman she should *expect* the crazy things to happen. "You're going to do some things that aren't like you at all," she said.

Then she reminded the woman, "That's okay. After all, you're NOT yourself right now. You're hurting, and you're lost. So don't be too hard on yourself when you lose the house keys or pay the phone bill twice or put salt in your tea or forget where you parked your car. Be patient with yourself. Gradually, your upside-down world will right itself, and you'll find your life returning to almost normal."

Every cloud has a silver lining. And sometimes a blot of
lightning.

I have wandered away like a lost sheep; come and find me for I have not turned away from your commandments. (PSALM 119:176 TLB)

"THAT'S THE TV REMOTE CONTROL YOU'RE HOLDING, NOT THE GARAGE DOOR OPENER."

I'd like to live life in the fast lane, but I'm married to a speed bump.

December 19

Let the little children come to Me, and do not forbid
them; for of such is the kingdom of heaven.
(MATTHEW 19:14 NKJV)

The youngest children enrolled in a church preschool always steal the show at the annual
Christmas program. Last year the children—none of
whom could yet read—held up brightly colored three-
foot-high placards that spelled out Christmas words.
The highlight came when one foursome walked on-
stage in reverse order and proudly spelled

RATS

Christmas is when God came down from heaven with a
baby in His arms.

Then you will call out, and the LORD will answer. You will cry out, and he will say, "Here I am." (ISAIAH 58:9 NCV)

What if God had an answering machine?

"Hello, thank you for calling heaven. Please select one of the following four options: Press 1 for requests, 2 for thanksgiving, 3 to complain, or 4 for all other inquiries."

No matter what you press, you hear, "All angels are helping other members of God's family right now. Please stay on the line, and your call will be answered in the order it was received.

"To find out how many angels dance on the head of a pin, press 5.

"If you would like King David to sing a psalm for you, press 6.

"To find out if your relative is here, enter his or her date of death and then listen to the list that follows.

"To confirm your reservation, press the letters J-O-H-N and the numbers 3-1-6."

Thank goodness we have God's promise that He is THE Operator who is always standing by!

Cordless phones are great. If you can find them.

December 21

Early in the morning, before the sun is up, I am praying and pointing out how much I trust in you.
(PSALM 119:147 TLB)

During this ultra-busy time of year, many women find that the quiet hours before dawn give them a time alone to pray and study and plan. I've always been an early riser, so when someone sent me a list of early risers in the Bible I was cheered by the thought that the time of day I love so much has always been a special time for God's children. If you're reading this during the predawn hours on a frosty December morning, I hope you're encouraged by realizing you're continuing a godly tradition that began centuries ago. For example, Exodus 34:4–5 describes Moses arising early in the morning to climb Mount Sinai, where he met the Lord, who had "descended in the cloud" (KJV).

No matter when you do it, make time each day during this hectic season to honor the *reason* for the season, who may have been born in the early hours of the morning.

You will never truly enjoy Christmas until you look into the face of the Father and tell Him you have received His Christmas gift!

God never changes his mind about the people he calls and the things he gives them. (ROMANS 11:29 NCV)

"That better not be my Christmas present!"

One child is not enough, but two children are far too many.

December 23

I was trembling with fear; all my bones were shaking.
(JOB 4:14 NCV)

One of the scariest things some men do is accompany their wives to the mall, especially at Christmastime, when the traffic is hectic and the stores are packed. One researcher said the stress levels in some men skyrocket when they're faced with crowded stores. The scientist compared it with the heart rate and blood pressure "you would expect to find in a fighter pilot going into combat."

Knowing how stressful it can be for Bill, I insist on driving when he accompanies me to the mall. I've adapted a strategic plan someone suggested for finding a parking space. What you do is hang your head out the car window . . . be very quiet . . . and listen for a motor to turn over. Then you tear across the parking lot in the direction of the sound, driving *against* the arrows, to try and get to that space first. Other than someone dying and leaving you a parking spot, I don't know of any other way to get one during the holiday rush.

Men are like parking spaces. All the good ones are already taken—and the rest are handicapped or their meters are running out!

And suddenly there was with the angel a multitude of the heavenly host praising God and saying: "Glory to God in the highest, / And on earth peace, good will toward men!" (LUKE 2:13–14 NKJV)

Someone told me about attending a holiday church service late on Christmas Eve in a beautiful old church in the midst of a large city's tall buildings and office towers. When the Christmas Eve service ended just after midnight, the churchgoers emerged through the old wooden doors to find snowflakes swirling through the air and the heart of the usually bustling city extraordinarily quiet. Suddenly the church's bells pealed out through the darkness, filling the empty streets with the glad tidings of Christmas, their joyful sounds echoing off the neighboring structures of concrete and steel. It was, my friend said, a most breathtaking moment, one she doesn't expect to equal until she hears those joybells of heaven pealing out a welcome to her.

Don't you hear those bells now ringing? Don't you hear the angels singing? 'Tis the glory hallelujah jubilee!

December 25

When the wise men saw the star, they were filled with joy. They came to the house where the child was and saw him with his mother, Mary, and they bowed down and worshiped him. They opened their gifts and gave him treasures of gold, frankincense, and myrrh.
(MATTHEW 2:10–11 NCV)

If God had a refrigerator,
     your picture would be on it.
If God had a wallet,
     your photo would be in it.
He sends you flowers every spring
     and a sunrise every morning.
When you want to talk, He'll listen.
He could live anywhere in the universe,
     and He chose your heart.
And that Christmas gift He sent you
     in Bethlehem?
Face it, friend, He's crazy about you!
     —MAX LUCADO

Happy birthday, Jesus!

Simeon . . . was a good man, very devout, filled with the Holy Spirit and constantly expecting the Messiah to come soon. For the Holy Spirit had revealed to him that he would not die until he had seen him—God's anointed King. The Holy Spirit had impelled him to go to the Temple that day; and so, when Mary and Joseph arrived to present the baby Jesus to the Lord in obedience to the law, Simeon was there and took the child in his arms, praising God. "Lord," he said, "now I can die content! For I have seen him as you promised me I would. I have seen the Savior you have given to the world."
(LUKE 2:25–31 TLB)

Like old Simeon I, too, "can die content," knowing that thrilling happiness awaits me in heaven. I'll be joining God and Jesus, and I'll also see my two boys. A friend wrote a beautiful poem for me about that day. The last two lines are my favorites:

> But when Gabriel blows his trumpet . . .
>   and when Toot and Scoot is here,
> Barb will jump the gate and grab her boys
>   as Jesus dries her tears.

Heaven: *No troubles. No trials. No tears!*

December 27

Jesus said . . . , "Go home to your friends . . . and tell them what wonderful things God has done for you; and how merciful he has been." (MARK 5:19 TLB)

**"OH, GLORY! OH, DELIGHT!
THE HOLIDAY HOUSEGUESTS HAVE GONE HOME!"**

He who is full loathes honey, but to the hungry even what is bitter tastes sweet. (PROVERBS 27:7)

I'm not sure that physical fitness is all that it's cracked up to be. A few years back, Bill and I decided to work on our mutual weight problem by increasing our aerobic exercise. We set up a regimen and tried not to miss it. Here's what we did: At night, we would walk to the Baskin Robbins ice-cream shop to have an ice-cream cone nightcap. And every morning we would walk to the Yum Yum Donut Shop for our usual hot coffee and warm maple bars. We really enjoyed these workouts, but even though we stuck faithfully to this routine for several weeks, neither of us lost a single pound. Obviously, there's something these fitness gurus aren't telling us!

Here's a great incentive for doing sit-ups: *Put M&Ms between your toes!*

December 29

Look, he is coming with the clouds, and every eye will see him, even those who pierced him; and all the peoples of the earth will mourn because of him. So shall it be! Amen. (REVELATION 1:7)

When Jesus comes again, every person on earth will see "the Son of Man coming on the clouds of the sky, with power and great glory. And he will send his angels with a loud trumpet call, and they will gather his elect from the four winds, from one end of the heavens to the other" (Matthew 24:30–31).

Thinking of that day, my heart beats faster, and my mind soars heavenward. Charles Wesley's hymn "Lo! He Comes, with Clouds Descending" perfectly captures my heart's desire:

> O come quickly, O come quickly!
> Alleluia! Come, Lord, come!

Sometimes when I'm humming that beautiful tune, I add my own little petition: *Lord, despite all the times I've been splattered on the ceiling, I've enjoyed this life. I'm thankful, Lord, but I'm ready. As soon as I hear those first notes from Your mighty trumpet, I'll be on my way!*

I'm ready for liftoff!

We believe that Jesus died and rose again and so we
believe that God will bring with Jesus those who have
fallen asleep in him. (1 THESSALONIANS 4:14)

The book *A Place Called Heaven* retells one of the favorite stories of the late Peter Marshall, former chaplain of the U.S. Senate: A young boy who was dying from an incurable disease asked his mother, "What is it like to die? Does it hurt?"

His mother reminded him of what it was like when he had played hard all day and fell asleep on the sofa or in the car on the ride home from his grandparents' house. "When you awoke in the morning you were in your own bed because your daddy came with his big strong arms and carried you home. Death is like that," the mother told him. "You fall asleep here, and you wake up and find that your Father has carried you home."

Those who live in the Lord **never** **see each other for the last time.**

December 31

But one thing I do: Forgetting what is behind and straining toward what is ahead, I press on toward the goal. (PHILIPPIANS 3:13–14)

hink . . .

Of stepping on the shore and finding it heaven;

Of taking hold of a hand and finding it God's hand;

Of breathing a new air and finding it celestial air;

Of feeling invigorated and finding it immortality;

Of passing from storm and tempest to an unknown calm;

Of waking and finding you're Home!

Remember: *You may be older today than you have ever been before, but you're younger than you will ever be again!*

Other selections by Barbara Johnson

Did God Really Say That? (video)

In this lively video, Barbara shares her collection of hidden gems. She brings laughter to the live audience by encouraging them to think about the "sweet-by-and-by while stuck in the nasty now-in-now."

He's Gonna Toot and I'm Gonna Scoot

Sharing outrageous humor, rib-tickling insights, and inspiring, real-life examples, Barbara shows readers how to put life's trials into heavenly perspective. While we wait on Gabriel's horn to sound, Barbara gives women an eternal telescope with which to view their often difficult world.

I'm So Glad You Told Me What I Didn't Wanna Hear

Bad news about your children carries a triple whammy of pain, worry, and "where did we go wrong!" Drawing on her personal experience and the letters she has received from hundreds of hurting women, Barbara shares hope and humor to encourage parents in seemingly hopeless situations.

More from The Geranium Lady...

Leaking Laffs Between Pampers and Depends

Grab your giggle box! Here comes
Barbara Johnson with another helping
of joy for women of all ages, aches,
and "architecture." You'll laugh at
Barbara's quirky strategies for empty-
nest de-cluttering, husband-handling,
kid-corralling, and parent-parenting.

Living Somewhere Between Estrogen and Death

From savoring the "here and now" to
preparing for our glorious future in
Heaven, Barbara offers a delightful recipe
for living life to its fullest in your later
years and spices it up with loads of laughter. In her familiar zany style, Barbara
shows women how to survive growing
older with courage and joy.

Mama, Get the Hammer! There's a Fly on Papa's Head!

Barbara insists that laughing in the face
of adversity is not a form of denial, but a
proven tool for managing stress, coping
with pain, and maintaining hope. She
zeroes directly in on the spiritual benefit
of a smile, a giggle, and a good,
old-fashioned belly laugh.

More from The Geranium Lady...

Pack Up Your Gloomies in a Great Big Box, Then Sit on the Lid and Laugh!
This book is filled with bittersweet stories of Barbara's journey through the minefields of life, and her wise and encouraging responses to letters from hurting parents. Each chapter ends with a laughter-packed collection of Gloomee Busters.

Splashes of Joy in the Cesspools of Life
Barbara's approach to life is positive, uplifting, therapeutic, and fun. This book offers an invigorating spurt of encouragement and a gentle reminder to splatter joy into the lives of others.

Stick a Geranium in Your Hat and Be Happy!
This is the book that started it all! Sharing her own difficult experiences, Johnson proves that while pain is inevitable, misery is optional. This powerful book has sold more than 1 million copies and made Barbara a perennially best-selling author.